PRAISE FOR

Women on Fire

BOOK AND TEA PARTIES

"*Margaret Mead once said, 'Never doubt that a small group of thoughtful, committed citizens can change the world . . . it is the only thing that ever has.' And I would add, "especially a group of women." Women are a powerful lot. We are the creators of change. And when we get to work, we make great things happen. Thank you, Debbie, for creating a venue where women can gather to make great things happen not only in their own lives, but in the lives of others.*"

~ Jennifer M. Granholm, Governor of Michigan

"*Where was this book 30 years ago when I was starting out? A welcome reminder that you gain more from adversity and failure than success!*"

~ Erin Moriarty, CBS News correspondent

"*This book is an inspiring, motivating treasure of women's triumphs over their challenges. It is destined to be placed on every woman's bookshelf right between* **Chicken Soup for the Women's Soul** *and* **Eat, Pray, Love**."

~ Dr. Ranjana Pathak, corporate vice president
and creator of www.ombics.com

"*Debbie Phillips's inner flame burns so brightly that all who surround her are caught up in the conflagration. In* **Women on Fire** *she has assembled a luminous group to tell their inspiring stories, ones that move us and challenge us to reach farther than we thought possible.* **Women on Fire** *is testimony that, if we continue to nurture the inner spark, it cannot help but ignite powerful transformation. Debbie is a nurturer of sparks. She should be forced to wear a sign that says, "DANGER: HIGHLY EXPLOSIVE HERE."*"

~ Edward L. Beck, ABC News correspondent
and author of *Soul Provider: Spiritual Steps to Limitless Love*

"This book answers the need of women everywhere who seek the empowerment and support Debbie Phillips so graciously creates as she tends the embers of the heart with such love and skill at her **Women on Fire** gatherings. Every woman, whether leader, entrepreneur, social activist, partner or mother will join this ever-expanding circle and be immediately enriched in making her own dreams come true."

~ Ellen Wingard, executive coach and co-author of *Enlightened Power: How Women Are Transforming The Practice of Leadership*

"**Women on Fire** will light your fire! Debbie has done wondrous work in bringing together women of like minds and souls. We are reminded that we never have to do it alone and that we are all part of each other's inspiration and support. All of our gifts are so needed now. It is no time to hold back. Let's light our fires!"

~ Agapi Stassinopoulos, speaker, author of *Gods and Goddesses in Love*

"A **Women on Fire** tea party is an enchanted journey into a mystical, magical place where very real life conversations happen, very real life chance meetings occur and very real life miracles abound. Debbie Phillips is Merlin in pearls!"

~ Gina Otto, author of *Cassandra's Angel*

"You deserve to be a **Woman on Fire** in your life. You deserve to read this delicious gem of a book, in which real women share how they left behind ordinary lives for lives of courage, fun, magic and true success. You'll find a dynamic support group in these pages!"

~ Tama J. Kieves, best-selling author of *This Time I Dance! Creating the Work You Love*

"**Women on Fire** is full of the richness of voices of women who have lived life, awakened to a deeper part of themselves and are ready to share their wisdom with one reader at a time. I laughed, I cried, I cheered and I felt the stories deep in my heart. The only thing better would be an in-person connection at one of Debbie's tea parties."

~ Andrea Hylen, co-author of *Conscious Choices: An Evolutionary Woman's Guide to Life*

"I have written that women are given poor advice when they are told to join an all-women network. And there's research to show women are more backstabbing to other women than to men. So it's great to see that Debbie Phillips is tackling the problem head-on by creating **Women on Fire** and environments where women can connect in positive, productive and useful ways. It's about time."

~ Penelope Trunk, entrepreneur, columnist and author of
Brazen Careerist: The New Rules For Success

"At the heart of authentic female wisdom are the values of collaboration, support, and generosity. When these attributes are present true community and inspired leadership follow naturally. **Women on Fire** and its author Debbie Phillips are both the living embodiment of this ancient wisdom that we so urgently need in these difficult times.

"As I read this book I felt like I was sitting in a circle of wise women warmed and emboldened by the fire of their passion, highest aspiration, and courageous action. With its lively style, fearless stories, and mandate to live your dreams no matter what, **Women on Fire** is the perfect antidote in our gloomy and disempowered climate."

~ Gail Straub, Co-Founder, The Empowerment Institute and author of
Returning to My Mother's House: Taking Back the Wisdom of the Feminine

"Thanks to Debbie Phillips's personal coaching and her **Women on Fire** tea parties, I am launching a travel website. I figured it was high time to do what I love. What a concept! Even though these are tough times to start any business, I will be well-positioned when the economy turns around. Best of all, I'm energized and excited about what I'm doing rather than drained and anxiety-ridden. I wish for everyone who reads this book to fulfill their dreams—even if the idea seems a bit crazy!"

~ Doni Belau, founder/creator/CEO, GirlsGuideToParis.com

"With **Women on Fire,** Debbie has created an environment where you are completely transported to a place of energy, possibility and support; where total strangers become instant friends, and treat each other as if it's always been so. And the impact of the experience lingers long after the party has passed. I find I can access the powerfully positive intentions of the women who gather in this group by simply recreating the event in my mind. What an honor to be included!"

~ Jenifer Madson, financial success coach and author of
A Financial Minute

"To really appreciate what **Women On Fire** is all about you must first know about the founder, Debbie Phillips. Debbie has been my personal coach and friend for more than five years, and I cringe to imagine where I'd be today without her advice, support and care. Because of Debbie's influence I developed the courage and dedication to follow my dreams of coaching, speaking and writing. Every time I doubted myself, felt like giving up, her calm, powerful voice gently put me back on track.

"Debbie is a natural connector, and when she first told me of the **Women on Fire** tea parties I knew it would be life changing for any woman who attended. When I went to my first WOF tea party in Los Angeles, I invited seven of my coaching clients to attend as well. Three of my clients met and created new close friendships from that one party; one started a joint-venture partnership, and all of them are looking forward to attending the next one. I personally got re-inspired to finish my book after attending, and made friendships with other women who wanted to help me promote my book to their contacts.

"As a coach, I know that much of success is due to whom we consistently rub elbows with, and being a member of **Women on Fire** myself, I have total certainty and confidence in where I am going because of the awesome support I have received and will continue to give and receive on this journey. I've witnessed too many women who make the mistake of trying to go for their dreams alone. It doesn't work that way, and it isn't any fun either! We need and deserve a team.

"Thank you, Debbie, for being in my life and following your vision for **Women on Fire!**"

~ Mandy Pratt, coach and co-author *Rich Coach, Broke Coach*

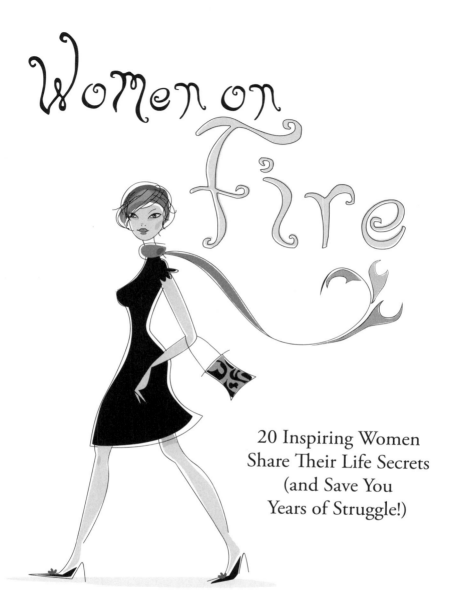

Women on Fire

20 Inspiring Women Share Their Life Secrets (and Save You Years of Struggle!)

DEBBIE PHILLIPS

Love Your Life Publishing
Dallastown, PA

Women on Fire: 20 Inspiring Women Share Their Life Secrets
(and Save You Years of Struggle!)

Published by:
Love Your Life Publishing, Inc.
PO Box 2, Dallastown, PA 17313
www.LoveYourLifePublishing.com

ISBN: 978-0-9820477-8-1
Library of Congress Control No: 2009924034

Cover design, layout and typesetting by Cyanotype Book Architects
Editors: Kacy Cook and Marlene Oulton
Author Photo: Jinsey Dauk

Printed in the United States of America

 Printed on recycled paper

A portion of the proceeds from this book will be donated to causes and
charities Women on Fire™ supports.

www.AboutWomenonFire.com

Dedication

For

Irene O'Garden, Kathleen Laughlin and Judith Ivey

Playwright, filmmaker, actress

Your brilliance led us to ours.

20 Aspirations of Women on Fire™

Are you a Woman on Fire? Ask yourself the following.

Do I:

- Desire deep fulfillment in my work and life?
- Cheer on the successes of other women?
- Embrace my talents and achievements?
- Eagerly share my information, ideas, experience and connections to benefit others?
- Always work to improve myself?
- Love to learn new things?
- Know how to ask for help?
- Invest in myself and my potential?
- Connect with other women in a trusting, soul-satisfying way?
- Have a positive attitude (at least 90 percent of the time!)?
- Have an awareness of my powerful impact on others?
- Dedicate myself to using my strengths, gifts and talents to make a difference in the world?
- Act in a clear, direct way with compassion and kindness?
- Appreciate, honor, credit and celebrate those who helped me along the path to my goals?
- Know (mostly!) when to say "YES!" and how to say "NO"?
- Cultivate a "tough mind" yet lead my life with a "tender heart"?
- Work toward my next desires and know that I am on my way, even if I may not yet fully know "how to get there"?
- Recognize my creativity as a gift to be protected, valued and nurtured?
- Give—and accept—love and support?
- Believe there is plenty in this world for me?

Table of Contents

Foreword

JANETTE BARBER

I once read that if you were to take a drop of pond water and view it under a microscope you would see, in microcosm, the entire pond. I believe that also holds true with people.

We see in each person's story all of our stories. That is what makes the individual accounts in this book so important. There is a part of all of us in these reflections. We have all dreamed and we have all achieved and we have all been on fire about something.

What Debbie Phillips gives us is the chance to be on fire together. Connecting gives us a way to recharge our own dreams and our own belief that we can achieve by bonding with other women in celebration of our goals, whatever they are. One thing I've learned is that when we "burn" together, the fire gets so much brighter.

I found Women on Fire by accident. I was at the first of the now-famous Women on Fire Tea Parties. (If you say to yourself, "Famous? I haven't heard of it." Well…I can't be responsible for that, can I?) The Tea Party is famous among the women on fire.

It's where small groups of us come together to meet other women and celebrate success by drinking tea and eating cakes. At the tea party, it becomes clear that success is really already yours and that everything imaginable is within the realm of possibility (including chocolate-covered strawberries, scones and clotted cream…).

It was September 2004 and my friend Agapi Stassinopoulos was in town promoting her book, *Gods and Goddesses in Love*. She had invited me to her press luncheon, which was lovely, and then she said to me, in her wonderful Greek accent, "Dahling, come to a tea party with me." I thought, "Good! There'll probably be tea." Little did I know. We walked into Lady Mendl's Tea Parlor on Irving Place in New York City, and as soon as I crossed the threshold I felt like Alice going through the looking glass.

Inside, it's elegant and Victorian. It was immediately clear that I had mystically left New York City and had time-warped into someplace that still had manners. For example, there isn't a coat room where you have to stand like herd animals waiting for your turn. Instead a well-dressed, soft-spoken, handsome young man in a suit will take your coat for you. Nice.

In this distinctive atmosphere, I met Debbie Phillips for the first time. Debbie feels like the most wonderful harbor you could ever imagine sailing into. She sets the tone. If you have never been to a Woman on Fire tea party, it's very hard to describe. On the one hand, nothing happens. On the other hand, everything happens.

Through these tea parties, Debbie Phillips has created a movement about women connecting with women. A Women on Fire tea is a place where women share their strength and their dreams and open the door to becoming who they had always intended to be but maybe forgot somewhere along the way. It's a place where growth is inevitable and transformation happens.

All my life I've been hearing about the "Old Boy Network"—that mysterious patchwork of men who are supposed to be able to shift lives and careers with a slap on the back and a handshake. Well, women definitely have to fight to find a place in the old boy network, so for myself, I'd rather skip that battle.

I'd rather be part of a new network of Women on Fire. Imagine! A world where every major city you go into has a Women on Fire network to plug into! That could so easily happen because Debbie Phillips definitely has a mission—to connect with other women and not to be satisfied until every woman can raise her own voice with authenticity and satisfaction and know that she is living her best life.

That is what it is to be a Woman on Fire. It means that you are ready to open, to connect and to grow. Join us. Together we will be a conflagration!

Introduction

First, a little quiz.

"Women on Fire" describes a:

- Documentary film
- One-woman play
- Book
- Tea party
- Retreat
- Coaching group
- Movement of fabulous women coming together to inspire, strategize and support each other's dreams
- All of the above.

Of course, because you are very smart and quite possibly a woman on fire yourself, you probably answered "all of the above." And you are correct!

The documentary film and the one-woman play I can take absolutely no credit for. In fact, I owe much to filmmaker Kathleen Laughlin for her delightfully quirky documentary of women discussing their experiences of menopause. I adored the movie and was enchanted upon meeting Kathleen. What dazzled me though was hearing the words "women on fire." Those three words strung together buzzed. They *felt* exciting, as though anything were possible if you were a woman on fire!

Several years later, I again met up with those stunning words. In a chance encounter at the Omega Institute in Rhinebeck, N.Y., I came upon playwright Irene O'Garden and her captivating one-woman play *Women on Fire*. In it actress Judith Ivey plays a dozen passionate women on the brink of self-discovery, all burning with her own personal fire. When I spoke with Irene, she not only opened her beautiful creative heart, but she also encouraged and helped me to follow my dreams of providing forums for women to flourish in.

Neither Kathleen nor Irene had known of the other and her "woman on fire" work. Generously, they both gave me their blessing to use the name "women on fire" in anything I'd create to uplift, benefit and transform the lives of women.

They are who I was thinking of when I wrote the Women on Fire aspiration of abundance: "I believe there is plenty in this world for me!"

Have you ever wondered just how great and deeply fulfilled you could be if only you had the inspiration, strategies and support to live up to your life's highest calling?

One of my favorite quotes from the Talmud is "Every blade of grass has its angel that bends over it and whispers 'grow, grow.'" Have you ever wished for your own angel to whisper over you like that?

Chances are you have. I certainly did.

From the beginning of my career, I held fascinating and creative jobs. I've been a radio and newspaper reporter, a presidential candidate's deputy press secretary and a governor's press secretary, and I've run a television production company.

I have loved my work, but I often felt I could somehow be better, truer to myself, less prone to falling into traps or stumbling through mistakes and stressing myself to a breaking point.

In all my jobs, I was surrounded by talented people—both men and women—and I learned a lot from them. Many even saw promise in me and cheered on my success. What I longed for, though, was someone to help me to become my very best in every way, personally and professionally.

In particular, I wanted women as role models so I could learn to lead with my own brand of feminine gifts, strengths and talents. Back in the 1980s, there were so few I related to, and the ones I did were out of my reach: Gloria Steinem and Hillary Rodham Clinton (much softer and quite witty when I initially met her as First Lady of Arkansas) were two.

So after more than 20 years in the workforce, I allowed my heart to lead the direction of my career. I simply created for other people what I had wanted for myself—someone to help me clarify and express my greatest gifts, strengths and talents in the world. It was several months before I found out my new endeavor had a name: I was an executive and life coach.

The profession was so new and unknown in 1995 when I started my practice that many people on hearing about it thought I had become involved in sports! Few understood how I could possibly make a living by supporting other people to stretch and be their best. But I did, and I was financially successful from the beginning.

Many people could not understand why someone would need—or even want—such a coach. True then, but not now.

Coaching took hold in the United States and around the world as more and more people experienced the value of this type of partnership. Today, there are tens of thousands of coaches. A *Harvard Business Review* study in 2009 revealed the meteoric rise in coaching. A decade prior, coaches were mostly hired to fix toxic behavior in employees. Now, coaches are more likely to be hired to help people develop their natural abilities and best qualities.

After several years of working one-on-one with professional women from all over the country, I was led to a dream of my own: I wanted to connect my wonderfully engaging, fabulous, talented clients with each other!

Even though each had me as her coach, I believed they would greatly benefit from knowing each other. "A rising tide lifts all boats" is one of my favorite sayings, and I felt if my clients knew one another's struggles, hopes and dreams, even greater joys would come.

So I finally revisited my three favorite words and started my own version of Women on Fire™. At first we held a large event, then a smaller day-long coaching group, and then tea parties, which turned out to be a big hit!

Over time, my clients began to invite their fabulous women friends to the tea parties, and those women invited their friends, and on and on it went. Today, Women on Fire has expanded and includes tea parties, retreats, coaching groups, Vision Days® (strategic life-planning days), videos and now this book.

"Grief shared is halved; and joy shared is doubled" is one of the reasons I wanted to create this book. I personally invited the authors within to share the deeply personal and powerful stories of their lives. When you see how another woman led the way or coped with or survived issues many of us have faced or may face over a lifetime, we grow stronger and smarter together.

I welcome you to join our circle of dynamic and authentic women. Any time you need a little inspiration or perhaps a strategy or some support and comfort, may you find it waiting for you in these pages.

We hope this book saves you some wear-and-tear so you can use the extra energy to create a life you really want and dream of.

It will be a great pleasure if one day I get to meet you and hear what you are "on fire" about in your life!

Debbie Phillips
February 15, 2009

PART ONE

Inspiration

Taking Shopping Seriously

How I almost overlooked a career that fits me hand-in-glove

 HOLLY GETTY

I work for a very large insurance company. Monday through Friday, I review accident claims, assess the damage to automobiles and file reports. I complete about 30 forms a day, talk to clients on the phone, and start my lunch countdown at about 11:15.

Oh, and I doodle a lot.

Wait, I'm sorry. What am I doing? I'm writing about a life the way my father planned it. Hang on! This is supposed to be about *my* life, the way *I* planned it. Sorry, I got confused for a second.

You see, Dad wanted me to be safe and insured...and then happy. Or not, but safe and insured for certain. It was a dad thing and a thing from his generation. He worked for one very large insurance company for 37 years. One life, one job. That was how you did it.

Day one of 1968, enter one daughter with little or no interest in anything insured, or even numeric, really. Dad loved me dearly and was charmed by my interests, but he couldn't identify with a single one of them.

You see, I grew up in the brown bathroom. Owned it. Claimed it at a very young age.

CREATIVITY CENTER

At 7, I reluctantly shared the space with my younger brother. I took over the faux marble countertop and claimed the far end as my makeshift

21

vanity. The poor kid had about eight inches of storage space, and I would pitch a fit if he stayed in the bathroom for more than 15 minutes.

This was my workspace. My creative home. Here, I used every potion and lotion I could find to make magic—braid my hair, cover my friend in makeup or make gifts for my mom.

A friend and I often rooted around in the gigantic linen closet of the previously mentioned, said brown bathroom to find ingredients to create things from. The closet was big enough to stand in, and we would hunt until something struck our fancy. One day, it was a box of tampons.

Not having a clue as to what they were, we experimented. I unwrapped the tubes, pulled the cords and submerged them in the sink. They expanded to five times their original size! Hours of fun.

Tying them onto a hanger, we sprayed the distended objects thoroughly with Love's Baby Soft—my fragrance of choice at the moment. Days later, they dried (in retrospect, probably many days later). As I held about eight in my hand, we tied the strings together, finished with a bow, wrapped them up in a box and, *voilà!* We were ready to give our mothers their own custom-made drawer sachets. Really? Yes, really.

I remember only that Mom's hand quickly muffled her involuntary scream as she opened the box. Scented, dried tampons with a bow. Shocking, maybe. But please, at age 7, this was genius…or, at least, pretty damn creative.

I'm sure you're thinking, "My God! Get this girl into an advanced beauty school immediately. We have a savant on our hands! If she can turn dried tampons into an attractive and useful gift, what other kinds of highly developed beauty skills must she possess?"

I hear ya.

Well, it wasn't that easy.

All I wanted to do was go to beauty school. Truly, it's all I ever really remember wanting to do. Dad would joke, "Yeah, you can go to beauty school after you graduate." After college graduation, I would ask, "*Now* can I go to beauty school??" "No," Dad would say, "I meant after you get your master's degree."

It was a big joke in the Getty household and, after so much time mocking my "talent," I saw it as a joke, too. Here is Holly. All she wants to do is play with makeup and lotions and shop. She doesn't want to do anything serious. She just wants to make people look better.

TAKING A SHINE TO SHOPPING

What 12-year-old do you know who buys clothes for herself, much less for her mother, father and brother? I could do it with my eyes closed. But instead of seeing it as a gift for fashion, it was seen in another way: I could make money disappear.

So the journey began. It's almost comical when I look at it now. There I would be, agonizing over what I was going to do with my life, when my mom would announce that she needed an outfit for a formal event. In about 10 minutes, I'd have her in the perfect cocktail attire, complete with clutch, shoes and earrings. Mom was thrilled and amazed at my ability. Then, I was back to my teenage angst (dramatic neck arch with hand on forehead): "Oh, whatever will I do with my life?"

I lived for the days when Mom and I would drive to Philadelphia to get haircuts and then spend the rest of the day at the King of Prussia mall. I would bound out of bed, ready to go early. Mom, God bless her, would just try to make it through the day. She loathed shopping, but so graciously indulged me with the time and space to shop all day—an enormous sacrifice. And she always complimented me and acknowledged my interest and taste. I flitted through the store, knowing she would be parked in the nearest chair. It was touching to me then and even more touching now.

I would spend hours at makeup counters asking about the latest exfoliator and in specialty stores wanting to know about the newest cut in jeans. Mom would shrink in embarrassment. "You're taking too much of their time. We have to buy something." I wanted to know more about everything. I was in my element. I didn't want to bother anyone; I just wanted to learn about it all.

I would end up buying so much stuff—way more than I needed or wanted (well, I thought I wanted it). The routine was always the same: I would sneak the bags into the house while my mother distracted my dad. Over a period of the next few days, I would gradually show him what I bought, explaining how new and different every item was and why it was a good purchase. Seeking his approval, for some unknown reason.

The whole process was infused with shame. I embarrassed my mother in the store, and Dad would get upset because I spent too much money, which I most certainly did. And then the American Express card would arrive. Oh, the horror.

So I never saw my passion for shopping as a gift. It was more like a disreputable compulsion. I did not embrace it, and I most certainly did not imagine it could be a career.

My mother saw it. She understood I had something special. Every time we shopped, she would say, "If you could just bottle it and sell it...."

My father would then say, "Yeah, you want to hurry up with that. I have an AmEx bill here."

My dad had plans for me. First and foremost, they were to get an MRS degree as quickly as possible. Go to college and leave with a degree in whatever—and a husband. That was Roger Getty's Plan A.

Plan B, an even more frightening possibility to me at the time, involved an entry-level job with his employer, the very large car insurance company. Imagine me, the girl born to bring out your bone structure, instead inspecting your car's front-end damage. I'm more interested in fingernail polish color and the lighting options of a makeup mirror. Working in insurance would have been a nightmare for me. The dear company and I both dodged a bullet.

I guess I could have applied for a beauty school scholarship (the tampon story alone would get me in, I'm sure) and worked my way through. But I saw my talent as a joke, as a needless, frivolous thing that I abused.

What I did instead was to drift around...and around and around. I ended up with BA in psychology and another one in fine arts. At the end of my college career, I was panicked and had no idea what I wanted to do. So the obvious choice was...you've got it, more school. I went to graduate school initially to study photography and pursue an MFA. After a semester of photography, I ended up drifting into the education department. I connected deeply with the head of the department, who later became my adviser, and began a master's in art education. I liked art. I liked school. It seemed like a fit.

It was a great experience, but I lacked the passion of the other students. I wasn't sure teaching was for me. I tried it, along with a series of other odd jobs, but I felt like something was missing. I toyed with the idea of getting married to someone who was offering. I considered it only because I had no idea what I was doing with my life. I was lost.

NEW YORK STATE OF MIND

Then my best friend moved to New York City, and I visited her for a weekend. Sitting amongst the plush red walls of the Ziegfeld Movie Theater, I turned to her and asked, "Why am I not living here?" Never before had I seriously considered moving to New York, not even for one moment. I didn't even have it on my radar. But, for some reason, in that moment, it all became clear. It was like someone gently tapped me on the shoulder and whispered in my ear, "Move to New York City."

Two weeks later, I crashed at Laura's studio. I found a job the following Monday and an apartment on Tuesday. It was truly the easiest thing I have ever done. I blew up my air mattress, threw on a Jones suit and started my job as a receptionist at Jones apparel.

Little did I know that I was starting an affair with the new love in my life—New York City. It is the place where I found myself and came alive. It felt more like home than anywhere I had ever been.

My dear dad was less than thrilled. Here was his highly educated daughter working as a receptionist in the city he most disliked. (Remember when people didn't like New York? Well, my dad led the charge.) Regardless, he funded the project (bless him) and convinced himself I would be home in six months and then get married.

"Screw the lease, come home and marry Shane" was my dad's answer to all my New York stories. Be it boy issues or job issues, the answer was always the same. But it was not to be. I finally felt connected, and moving home was never a consideration.

I was "receptioning" my heart out for a couple weeks when a spot as a design assistant opened up at Jones. *Perfect*, I thought. I had it all figured out: I was in New York City, I loved to shop, and there I was working in design for a clothing company. Fabulous! I had found my passion. Clothing!

But not so fast. Although the world of clothing was interesting to me, "seeing how the sausage is made" showed me that retail wasn't the right fit either. I wanted to help people feel better. That is really what I always loved to do. But that was not the top priority in a frenetic business like retail. I was getting closer, but I still felt empty.

Even though it wasn't a perfect match, there was a flow. I was given job offers rather easily and, with each one, I felt it was to be my last, as surely my purpose would present itself soon and I would be freed from the indecencies I saw. Surely soon.

One low moment was while I was working at a start-up, which shall remain nameless, and by direction of my boss, I took a private car and her credit card to a well-known, pricey fashion house. My co-worker and I acted like we were a couple and bought thousands of dollars worth of clothes, whether they fit or not. We brought them back to the office, cut them into swatches, and the next day we presented them to the company that had created them as *our* product. I was shocked and disgusted to be a part of the process.

Despite my feelings, I didn't leave. Partly because I didn't know what else to do, and partly because there was some tiny part of me that felt like I needed to be there. I stayed in the industry, and soon my resume read like a mall directory: Lauren/Ralph Lauren, Jones, J Crew, Dana Buchman and Calvin Klein, to name a few. There were fantastic opportunities in the industry—some really great people and great experiences. Throughout my career, I traveled to Paris, Milan, Hong Kong, Tokyo, Osaka, Istanbul and Korea. It was a rare opportunity, and I loved the visual and cultural aspects of the job.

So much of it was a dream, but as I was moving from job to job in the fashion industry, my insecurities were growing. Focus was always on appearance, and I judged myself harshly. I was never thin enough, never cool enough. My inner critic was having a field day.

I couldn't accept myself, so I tried to pattern myself after a co-worker. Despite the fact that she was a foot taller than me, had an opposite body type and was completely different from me in just about every way, I copied her style. I was disconnected from myself, and the days were long, since I spent so much time beating up on myself.

BATTLING THE INNER CRITIC

I tried different approaches to reconnecting to my inner self: therapy, coaching and any class that would help. But finding my passion was not some sparkle-filled moment with harp music playing in the distance. I doubted myself deeply. I had so little faith in myself because of my shame that I really didn't think I had much to offer. Did I want to write? Work with dogs? Try advertising? I didn't have a clue.

I finally decided to focus all my energies into finding the right career. Whatever it took, I was going to find my passion.

I decided to follow my coach's advice and take a gestalt management class. As compelling as the class was, I could not take my eyes off of one of my classmates. In this rather exclusive and expensive class, there sat a man dressed like he was ready to rob a minimart.

Unshaven and unkempt, his off-putting appearance, I learned, had nothing in common with the person he was. He loved opera, had an extensive knowledge of wine and was sharp as a tack. From an affluent family, he had played the role of the black sheep. This class was a way for him to appease the family and, he hoped, help himself.

Out of someplace in myself I had not previously accessed, I told him I did not buy his look. I did not think this outer shell represented his depth.

Did I just think that or say it out loud? I asked myself.

I offered to give him a makeover, head to toe. If he paid for the services and the clothes, I would redo his look in a day.

Shockingly, he agreed. A facial, haircut, manicure, new glasses and shopping spree later, he appeared to the class as a new man. Perceptibly taller and suddenly handsome, he blew everyone away. He wore a jacket, sat tall and participated in class, something he had not ever done before. Everyone loved his new look, and I could see his confidence grow immediately. I was over the moon and marveled at how fun and easy it all was.

In the weeks to follow, he got a job and a girlfriend; again, things he had not done before.

Another classmate asked me to makeover one of his clients. Then another, and from there more. I found my passion and my voice all at once.

STAMP OF APPROVAL

Voice. In my family, my mother's voice wasn't heard enough. Dad was smart, temperamental, loveable and extremely witty. Mom, soft-spoken, sweet and extremely wise. Dad's temper overshadowed Mom's gentleness way too often, especially when she expressed appreciation for my interests. I really needed validation from my dad.

"Why do you need his approval?" Mom would ask. "You know he never will give it."

Here I was, a 33-year-old woman so desperate for her dad's approval of her business, a business that would have seemed something so foreign to him, so risky, so scary. There was no way in the world my father, with his background and his view of the world, would ever say, "Go, girl! We believe in you. You go get people to pay you to take them to a store. You do that. I believe in you!"

Never. Never ever. Never ever ever.

Instead, our phone calls ended with Dad saying, "Well, this shopping thing isn't going to pay the bills. Don't you dare let this affect your job."

"Give up the dream," Norman, my genius therapist, would tell me. Dad had his view, I had mine. It should have been enough.

Then something happened. My first business cards arrived and I was overjoyed. *Holly Getty, Personal Style Consultant.* I was sitting on a bench in Philadelphia with my parents, and I brought out the cards. Stiffening up, I was ready to hear my dad say they were a waste of money. To my surprise, he asked for a big pile of them. Mom said, "Don't take too many." And he replied in his usual temperamental way, "Goddammit, I'm proud of her, for chrissake."

Sure, it came with a few expletives, but that moment on the bench meant a great deal to me. Besides my dad's encouragement, it also reminded me how my mom's quiet belief in me was always there. She has more faith in me than I ever knew. She listens to my challenges, gives incredible advice and deeply believes in my gift.

Her voice gets stronger every day.

We lost Dad three years after the day on the bench. I miss him and I know, in his way, he was proud of me. I wish he could see what I have accomplished since then.

You see, I have become very serious. I am serious about what I do for my clients. I help them gain confidence to do what they are put here on this earth to do. When they discover their authentic style and allow what is inside to be reflected outside, their opinions of themselves change, too. It's a beautiful process, and it flows through me.

My opinion of myself has evolved, too. Today, I am more concerned with being warm than being cool, and I know that comes from the inside out.

HOLLY GETTY is known for helping people achieve their authentic, sustainable style while working within their budget. During her career in the fashion industry, she has worked for such notables as Liz Claiborne, J Crew and Calvin Klein. She has bachelor's degrees in fine art and psychology from Gettysburg College, a master's from Penn State and has done postgraduate work in Gestalt Psychology. For her free style tips, go to: www.hollygetty.com

A Queen in the Family

*How I kicked my eating disorder, shed harsh family scorn, pulled a
rabbit out of a hat and became a queen*

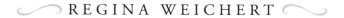 REGINA WEICHERT

I sweep into the room in a chiffon gown and lavender lamb boa. My
heart-shaped red rings sparkle, and I swirl about the children as I sing:

I am the Queen of Self-Esteem!
What does that mean?
I love myself!
I love myself!
I love myself!

Twenty-four nine-year-olds stare at me, stunned. Have they never seen
a queen in six-inch ruby platforms and a gold-sequined crown before?
I suck up their surprise and glow. I am Glinda the Good Witch of the
North come to slide ruby slippers on their spirits. I make self-esteem
something they'll never forget!

Just to be clear, this is my work. I have a performance character
called the Queen of Self-Esteem, and I use her to talk with people
about—yes—self-esteem. This leads folks to eye me and laugh. "Hey, you
must feel really great about yourself! Why do you do this?" And I laugh,
too. Because for 37 long years the torment of no self-esteem was mine. It
took all that time to rise above family messages that flattened and tattered
me to find my true place in life. How? By learning to love myself, and by
doing something I love doing.

MY MEASURING STICKS

My father is abandoned by his father. My grandfather runs off with
another woman during the Depression and leaves my grandmother alone
to raise three children. My father rises above his abandonment by acing
languages in the service and working for the CIA. At last he becomes a
famed surgeon. He's a millionaire and money his measuring stick—but
he wears humble suits and stockpiles cans of beans. "Be more, seem less,"
Dad says.

Ironman doesn't begin to describe him. During his training, he
works 90 hours on and 90 off. The great stress rots his teeth, but he keeps
going. A hunter, he wakes at 4 a.m. and heads for the Adirondacks, climbs
a pine tree, stays motionless for hours, bags a deer and later hangs the
wide-eyed beast in the garage to cure. For a snack, he slices strips of meat
off the carcass and feeds them to us raw with a grin and cackle of "venison
carpaccio." In his 70s, he falls 18 feet from a tree stand and breaks his
pelvis, shoulder, wrist and ribs. He also smashes his cell phone and all
hope of calling 911. So with bones splintered, he crawls to his tractor,
hauls himself up and drives back to his farm. On the way he crashes into
his neighbor's barn and splinters that too before the helicopter lifts him
off to the first of five surgeries.

He's so brilliant at cutting up things: his patients, animals, us. There
he goes, down the fall line—perfect and charming and icy. I am the oldest
of four children and the only girl. Dad gets on us about something and,
whatever our shame or silence or tears, he WILL NOT LET UP. He
attacks at random with words and fists—although, as a girl, I am spared
the fists. He reams me for reading aloud from a *New York Times* article
about the benefits of massage. Another time I'm reamed for how I make
pancakes. Answer back? Ha! He is King. But does he flay his harmless
daughter or some phantom from his youth?

My mother's family comes from Eastern Europe, and when they
arrive in Manhattan my grandmother Rivka goes to her first day of
school. The teacher tells her, "We don't have that name here," and calls
her Regina. My namesake dies before I am born, but leaves a whisper of
the Queen behind.

Like my father, my mother is a doctor, and she is an identical twin.

She gives me her love of art and fashion. I grow up reading *Vogue* with her. She points to a model: "Isn't she BEAUTIFUL?!" Under gloomy Syracuse skies, she is an Indian princess and stands out with her long sheen of black hair and exotic dress. She wears designers and palazzo pants and backless tops and gorgeous hot pink and a heaven-made turquoise silk party dress with bell sleeves! I adore her.

I don't have clothes; my mother won't buy them for me. She takes me shopping, but just buys for herself. Or she buys me the same thing she gets for herself but in a different color. Sometimes she gives me a gift, but strokes and pines over it until I just give it back to her. To have clothes, I borrow from her or my brothers. Her scrutiny of my body never stops. When I am 12 she begins pinching my thighs and telling me, "If you just lost five pounds, you'd be perfect." Looking at my size 10½ feet, my mother says, "If you lose weight your feet will be smaller. Fat deposits around the feet." But my feet grow on to their present size 11.

I am no fatter than any teen girl with a few extra pounds. This doesn't matter to my father, who calls me fat and mocks, "Women are weak."

FOOD FIGHT

I am a good girl and mother's helper and always at the top of my class. My two middle brothers get into boy-type scrapes—they shoot BBs at chipmunks and freak out neighbors who call the police! At age five my youngest brother, a free spirit and as beautiful as a girl, wears one of Dad's white T-shirts as a dress and capers down the street—a little ghost with skinny legs, no undershorts and the world's longest eyelashes. My brothers like to spy on me. After a shower, fed up at the rustling at the bathroom keyhole, I yank the door open in my dripping wet, naked glory and scream, "If you want to look, LOOK!"

The better I try to be, the worse off I am. Dad leaves to hunt and Mom doesn't like the woods, and never the twain shall meet. The pressure feels so great; something must break. More and more I am the cook as my mother steps aside and lets me do the kitchen work. I go to other families for comfort. I can't talk about what is going on at home, but it helps to know there are places where people are nice to each other.

I hole up in my room with Agatha Christie, Sherlock Holmes and other masters of deduction. By 15 I am a double agent and my mission is Bulimia. I teach myself to be a pastry chef and serve to my family sweets that I can't have myself. I could show you a picture of me with bulimia, face swollen and smile cringing above my mother's pale yellow T-shirt, jammed into Dad's belt and jeans borrowed from a young man who is staying with us that summer. All that's mine are a gold chain necklace and the cake I am holding—a whipped cream tower. It buckles with hand-cut chocolate diamonds and green lattice frosting and buttery hot-pink flowers. I could show you that picture, but I burned it.

For years I don't tell anyone about the bulimia—not my brothers, not my friends. When my parents find out, my father says, "Just stop." Being dutiful, I try, and fake my recovery. But I am far from recovered. When I ask to see a psychiatrist, my mother waves me off and says that I am going to college soon. Out of control, stressed down to the bone, menses irregular, I head off to Harvard.

Bulimia is a serial killer in your head that starves and tortures and mocks day in and day out. I am the victim and the killer. I never mean to hurt myself. But for seven years, the only thing I can do is fight with food.

I don't use laxatives or diuretics or alcohol, but at my worst I eat and vomit all day long. After a bad bout, I know that pushing it further will kill me. Luck strikes and, during my freshman year, I have a roommate whose father is a psychiatrist. He gives me a therapist's name and my healing begins.

I dream I am biking to the house I grew up in. The storm-lashed road sucks at the tires, and I slip and sense danger. I reach windows dark and broken: No one home. So I walk to my best friend's house next door, empty but dry. My mouth fills with broken glass. I can't swallow or cry out through the crushed shards. I just hold still and feel it. Will I die? No, my body has made special velvet mucus that coats my throat. I will get the glass out and be OK.

With much backsliding I trudge my way back toward reality. I master keeping food down no matter what I eat. I forgive myself if I cheat and throw up and just start each day fresh. I try to keep down the idea that I have some worth. Three things help me recover:

1. I believe that bulimia is not what I am but something I do.
2. I cling to the idea I can be healthy.
3. I reach out to others for help.

When I am 23 and just emerging from my illness, my youngest brother, William, tests positive for HIV. We are the two oddballs in the family and quite close. He hides being gay until he goes to college. His first boyfriend there gives him the virus. So at 17 William comes out as gay and HIV-positive at the same time. Forced to speed-bloom, he lives for 10 years. He finishes NYU, becomes a singer/songwriter and, in the last few years of his life, a drag queen.

LIGHTEN UP!

His drag name is Prissy La, and unlike most queens he writes and sings all of his own songs. He performs at USA, Webster Hall and other clubs in New York City. My father tells me, "Your brother is a dime a dozen— a homosexual with AIDS." But Prissy La is off doing high kicks in a red sequin miniskirt and singing, "Martha Stewart says to-mah-to not tomato/And if you try to argue she'll hit you with a ladle!" My brother says, "I like being a boy, and I like being a girl." Either way, his light shines!

For a long time I don't like drag. I think it demeans women. By this time my brother is ill, and I go to AIDS support groups. At one group, a gay man complains that drag queens demean gay men. I laugh and get the message that we should all lighten up and stop taking ourselves so seriously! I wonder, "What if a woman were a drag queen?"

William, dying, has brain changes and speaks verse from his world within. He twirls a perfect double Lutz from his teen ice-skating days, pats his leg to summon our long-departed black Lab and slides into a coma. *I dream that he gets out of bed healthy and aglow with a diamond teardrop on his brow. He's so happy, and cries, "I've got it! I've got it!"* A few days later he's gone. I lie down for a long time.

Back on my feet, I seek health with a vengeance. I am exhausted all the time and sick with flus that last for months. Later, helping others is a great spiritual reward. But first, I must learn compassion for myself. And I must get my bite back!

My acupuncturist says, "Like snakes, we all need our venom to digest our food. If we put our venom outside ourselves by throwing up, other things begin to feed on us." My osteopath's hands coax the bulimia pattern from my esophagus, and I go to bed for two days, a limp worm. My belly throbs, but endless visits to doctors and countless tests find only emotions in turmoil. At last I find the right specialist, and he unearths two intestinal parasites and a quite likely long-standing infection in my colon.

A trip to Africa gives me another parasite, but a nutritionist handles my recovery from colitis. Too weak to move for months, I must stop "doing." I live on homemade chicken soup and learn nurturing on a gut level. A jaw specialist gives me a splint for my mouth that wipes out my chronic pain in jaw, neck and shoulders. "Your teeth never grew fully down into your mouth," he says, "but don't worry. Your fangs will be good as new." In memory's kaleidoscope, it's only an instant, but in real time my recovery takes 25 years—sacrificed on the altar of the Bulimia god. Today I have the joy that at 46 I am pain-free and healed—a miracle I always believed in but did not feel worthy of.

A WING AND A PRAYER

Along the way, I have some dramatic visits from the Muse: *I dream an FBI agent tells me that William has been taken into the witness-protection program for people with AIDS and that they take only the strongest people. Then I am onstage performing in a gorgeous rainbow of color and music.* In waking life I struggle with an abusive job. *One night William drops in to give me a hug so real I smell him. He urges, "Let's get out!" He runs off into snowy woods and moonlight. I run after him.*

I go to Bergdorf Goodman to buy some stockings for a job interview. On the street outside this store in Manhattan's priciest district sits an African-American woman, naked except for a garbage bag, and about my age. I am upset. How can I help? Inside a saleswoman tells me that when the police come, the woman on the street puts on her clothes and walks away.

I feel a little better and stop in the hat department to try on a purple ostrich number that catches my eye. There I am in the mirror as I always wanted to be—with a feather in my cap! When I leave, the woman in the garbage bag is gone. I go to therapy and spend 45 minutes moaning about what to do with myself.

I visit a successful friend and afterward am beating myself up for not being more like her. Suddenly a song pops into my head: "I am the Queen of Self Esteem/What does that mean?" It stops my self-attack cold. So I decide to listen and go home to write it down.

I start performing with gowns inherited from my brother and a singer aunt, and with some zany colored hair and a wing and a prayer. Over time I create a workshop for children: "Self-Esteem: What's It Mean?" I use songs, stories, poems and creative activities to share ideas about self-esteem, self-criticism and self-protection.

I am lucky early on with performing. I feel connected to my child and adult audiences. People like me, so I have enough encouragement to keep going.

When I tell my father about my work, he snorts, "Do you really think you are a Queen? Do you think you are better than anyone else?" As usual, I fizzle before his scorn and power. So I never get to answer, "No, Dad, but if *I* can learn to have self-esteem, anyone can. The Queen is a character who presents an image of possibility: What if we could all have total self-esteem?" But he already has that by the bucketful—or has he?

My dying father fights his cancer up until his last week. I am in the hospital taking care of him when his doctor comments that my name means queen. Dad sighs, "Oh, she thinks she is, she thinks she is! Never name your child Regina!" During one death scare he calls to say goodbye and "Forgive me." I say, "I do, Dad, I do." His last day, he is a wizard blazing on the bed's edge with a white towel draped over his hips. He stares at me and whispers something I can't hear, but my brother tells me he said, "beautiful." I hold Dad's hand as he dies and don't let go until they come to take his body an hour later. At his funeral I meet many who tell me of his kindness and humor, that he never raised his voice in the operating room, that he was a gentle and excellent teacher. I am amazed and glad to hear this praise of my father—the great man I missed knowing.

My mother invites me to France and China. Do I dare to visit the capital of the fashion world and the Great Wall with her? It seems we still have a ways to travel together, so I say, "Yes."

Back in the fourth-grade classroom, we finish up and the children make shields of self-protection. One girl draws a flask of disappearing potion and its formula—one part skunk and one part eraser—"to make mean people vanish!" Another covers her shield with flames and the slogan "Burn the insults away." One student goes home to dress up as the Queen of Self-Esteem, saying, "The Queen is my hero, and I am going to think about how she would handle things." Another writes, "You changed my life. I felt bad and awful. I always thought I was not good at anything. Now I feel awesome, cool, and good at stuff." Years later I bump into a boy from the class, and he says, "We were just talking about you the other day. We still sing the song you taught us."

I dream of a queen. I am worried—did someone steal my idea? I have wasted so much time. Is it too late for me?! In answer, the queen hands me a long paper scroll wrapped around a silver rod and says, "I teach people to remember their future."

Self-esteem, pass it on!

REGINA WEICHERT received her B.A. from Harvard and M.F.A from the School of Visual Arts. She produced programs and communications for the Museum of American Folk Art, Museum of Modern Art, CBS, Dean Witter and other Fortune 500 companies. She first appeared as the Queen of Self-Esteem in 1999, and in 2005 founded the company

"Queen of Self-Esteem LLC" to create ground-breaking tools for helping people improve self-esteem. You may contact Regina at 917-863-4727 or www.queenofselfesteem.com

Finding Something to Wine About®

My journey from frustrated wine drinker to wine educator

 LAURIE FOSTER

It took one of the darkest days in our nation's history to shine a light on the path to following my passions, propelling me to make changes in my life and grow in my career beyond anything I could have imagined.

A change was not inevitable. Everyone thought I had the greatest job in the world. I made lots of money working as a sales executive for an Internet software company, traveling all over the country and working with some of the finest minds in the business. But somehow I felt something was missing. I wanted to feel more passion for my career and to connect with people in a deeper way. How to achieve this seemed a mystery to me.

One aspect of my job I enjoyed most was entertaining prospective clients, which typically meant taking them out to dinner and enjoying great food and wine. During those years, I had the privilege to dine in some of the finest restaurants in the United States. Sampling great wines was a joy for me, but ordering from a wine list was another story. Like people in many other suburban households in America, I did not grow up enjoying or learning about wine at the dinner table. In fact, as a child of the '80s, I was more exposed to wine coolers and wine that came in a box.

I will never forget the first time I was handed an extensive wine list. Everyone at the table was looking to me to choose the perfect wine selection to accompany our meal. I scanned the list for anything familiar and hoped the client could not see how nervous I was. On other occasions

I asked the waiter for help, but my requests were greeted with indifference or, worse yet, an attitude of snobbery. These experiences motivated me to start studying wine so I could navigate the wine list and dazzle my clients unassisted.

MERGING PASSIONS

I began taking wine classes, attending wine dinners and reading as much as I could about wine. If I could sell complex software to Fortune 500 corporations, there had to be a way to understand the world of wine. In the fall of 1999, I took a cooking class with Chef Michael Forster of Hampton's Restaurant in Baltimore. While I never learned to love cooking, I did fall in love with the chef.

When Michael and I began dating in early 2000, I was searching for another type of passion, one that would reinvigorate my life's work. Michael was very supportive of my search. One night over a bottle of Australian Shiraz, we realized that we both had always dreamed of touring Australia. In early 2001, we decided to make that dream a reality, and we both gave notice to our employers. By the end of January, we were on a three-week tour "down under." We tasted some of the best wines that the Hunter and Barossa valleys had to offer and visited some of Australia's finest restaurants.

We spent the last week of our trip at Copper's Beach in New Zealand. One evening as we strolled along the beach, Michael asked me to marry him. I was shocked yet delighted. I knew he was the person I was meant to spend my life with, so I immediately said yes. That night we started planning our new life together.

We decided that our new life as a couple would begin in New York City. What better place to pursue our passions? Michael had spent his early years as a chef working there and missed the energy and excitement of New York City kitchens. And I knew that there was no better place to pursue my two major passions—people and wine. In April 2001, we found a great apartment in lower Manhattan, where office buildings were being converted to residential housing units. Every subway line was accessible from there, and with the World Trade Center business district only four blocks away, we had lots of great dining and shopping to choose from. I spent the summer getting to know and love New York City, with its fabulous restaurants, expansive wine shops and educational opportunities on every block.

During that time, following my interest in helping people, I enrolled at Coach U and began exploring a career as a life coach. I took several classes and immediately began working with clients. As a coach I was able to help other people examine their own lives, to set goals and make choices that supported them in living happier and healthier lives. One area that constantly surfaced with my clients, especially women, was the need to take time for themselves, while also making time to create a network of friends for support. I found that the clients I worked with were so busy with career, family and partners, that they had no time to meet new people or even just have a night out to enjoy a quality meal and a nice bottle of wine.

TRAGEDY INSPIRES CHANGE

Then, on Sept. 11, my life changed forever, as it did for so many people around the world. The day started as a typical morning. As usual, we awoke late. Michael started the coffee as I slowly rolled out of bed and made my way to my morning cigarette. As I had done every morning, I thought to myself this would be a good time to get serious about quitting smoking. But this morning would be different. I heard a loud explosion and felt the apartment vibrate. I remember joking to Michael that maybe this was the first earthquake in the northeast.

I turned on the TV and watched in horror as the reporter announced that a plane had hit the World Trade Center. At the time, it was being reported as a commuter plane with apparent FAA system problems. We could already see billowing smoke from our window and papers streaming like in a ticker-tape parade. I still felt relatively calm and safe until I heard the second explosion, which seemed louder than the first. I ran to the TV to see footage of the plane hitting the second World Trade Center building. We decided it was time to head uptown.

As we emerged from our building, we could feel the tension in the air. People were unsure of what to do, where to go. We headed north, away from the World Trade Center, as fast as possible. Smoke billowed out of the buildings and filled the sky. Time stood still and each block seemed a mile long.

The street was packed and the crowd was moving quickly, but people were orderly. I remember hearing someone yell, "The tower just came down!" Then soon after, "Oh no! The second tower came down!" I was too scared to look back. As we walked on, it all seemed unreal. What was happening? How could this be? I remember thinking that all of us on this street walking for our lives were equal. It didn't matter who you were, what you did, or even how much money you had. We were all in this together.

We reached Michael's restaurant in midtown and sat in shock, watching news of the morning's events. It took a week to get back into our apartment, and our neighborhood remained closed to traffic for months. At first, I put all my plans on hold. But with the help of friends, family and my life coach, I came to realize that now more than ever I needed to find my passion. We had been so lucky that day to escape harm, and I wanted to make every day count.

In early 2002, I began the process of studying wine by embarking on a certification program for wine professionals with the American Sommelier Association. Because I was new to the world of professional wine studies, I completely immersed myself in learning and absorbing the material contained in the course. But during the six months it took me to complete my certification in viticulture and vinification, my previous feelings of intimidation about my lack of knowledge came rushing back. I felt that the wine education I was receiving was amazing, yet shouldn't it be more fun with fewer pretenses?

During this time, Michael and I were also planning our April wedding, which would include, as a theme, stations pairing various dishes with the wines we loved. We enjoyed planning the menu, selecting the wines and using our collective talents to create a fabulous evening for our guests. Each wine served had a special significance to us and our relationship—many from wineries we had visited in Australia.

LIFE'S WORK

Our wedding also helped to solidify my desire to make wine my life's work. I noticed our guests tasting and enjoying the food and wines at each station. People who, for example, had never tried a dry Riesling from Australia or grilled ostrich felt safe with our recommendations to experiment and enjoy. This brought me great joy, and I knew this was just the first of many food and wine events I would plan.

Following our wedding, we went to Italy for our honeymoon. We both loved Italian food and wine, and it was the perfect way to spend our first few weeks as husband and wife. We toured the wine regions of Piedmont and Tuscany, as well as the cities of Venice, Rome and Lake Como. In Piedmont, we visited wineries in Barolo and Barbaresco, where I felt a special connection with the people, the wines and our local guide.

When we returned from Italy, I completed my certification and began working as a sales consultant for the largest wine retailer in New York City, Astor Wines. My job was to assist people looking for anything from a $10 bottle of wine to high-priced wines that cost $100 or more. I learned that most people want to enjoy wine but feel that the jargon and pomp-and-circumstance leave them confused and frustrated. They all came to me looking for simplification, advice and, of course, a great bottle of wine. This was exactly what I had wanted since that the first day I was handed that extensive wine list and felt intimidated by it.

In May 2003, I was blessed with the birth of our daughter, Michaela, and made the decision to be a stay-at-home mom. Michael and I discussed leaving Manhattan in search of a slower-paced environment where we could have more space for Michaela. We got our chance when Michael found an executive chef position with an exciting new restaurant in Virginia Beach. I had to adjust not only to motherhood, but to an entirely new living situation as well. I loved being home with Michaela, but I missed having friends to share an evening out or an adult conversation. In an effort to meet other women, I joined a multitude of "mommy groups," but I was not able to find women who shared my passions.

That was when I came up with idea to hold wine-tasting events for women. I thought it would be wonderful to create a group that allowed women to come together and learn about wine in an attitude-free environment. In 2004, we moved back to Maryland, where I hosted my first women's wine dinner. My coach had helped me set the goal and take the necessary steps to make it happen. To generate interest, I walked around town with postcards I had printed at home. To my surprise, the dinner quickly sold out, and it was so much fun!

The next month, the local newspaper ran an article about my business, and it really took off. The women who came to my events each month loved learning about wine and having time away from their hectic lives. Further, these dinners created an opportunity for my guests (and me) to develop friendships and support each other along the way. This was exactly what I had been searching for! The word spread, and soon women from a neighboring city were asking me to host events there, too. I expanded and began offering events for corporate functions as well.

FINDING A UNIQUE NICHE

That is when the idea of The Wine Coach® came to me. I could blend my knowledge of wine with my experience as a life coach. My new goal was to help everyone connect with wine in a way that was approachable and fun, while also creating opportunities for them to bond with each other. At my events, guests begin by talking about the wine, but by the end they are having conversations about the important things in their lives—their families, their passions—and even trading phone numbers.

There is an old proverb that states, "Over a bottle of wine many a friend is made." I have found that learning about wine often teaches us broader lessons about life and gives us a safe place to begin connecting with others. Each event I hosted confirmed this, as I saw people expanding their knowledge of wine along with their circle of friends.

My business grew and I quickly learned how important it was to reach as many people as possible through various forms of media. In the fall of 2005, I was asked to start contributing to a magazine. Each month I wrote a column focused on a specific wine topic, along with suggestions for wines to try at home. I also began sending out weekly emails with a wine tip to my online subscription list, whereby readers would also learn about new events and tours. Although I had never thought of myself as a writer, I really enjoyed helping people learn about and, of course, enjoy wine more.

Throughout 2005, my event business was busy, but I really missed traveling and visiting wineries. I began thinking of putting together a wine tour so I could share that experience with the people who attended my events. I had kept in touch with our tour guide from our honeymoon trip to Piedmont, Italy, and thought she might want to partner with me to create a wine tour. At the same time, I received a call from a travel expert in my area who wondered if I would consider doing a wine tour! It seemed that the stars were in alignment, and I launched The Wine Coach® Tours in January 2006.

Since then I have led two wine tours of Piedmont, Italy. I love watching my guests experience how special Piedmont is, and my connection to the region deepens each time I visit. I also have expanded the tours division to include domestic wine tours as well as culinary cruises. Like mine, both my local guide and travel partner are women-owned businesses. Building the tours division would not have been possible without their skills, expertise and friendship.

I also launched a radio show in 2006. Ironically, this opportunity came while I was helping a friend publicize a book she had just published on women and finances. I set up a series of events to help her reach people in my area and, in advance, she called our local radio station to set up an interview to help publicize our book signing. The evening of her book signing I had an informal wine tasting to kick things off. Unbeknownst to me, the program director from WCEI, the local radio station, was there. After the event, we struck up a conversation, and I pitched the idea of a radio show about wine. By the following month, we began my weekly segment called "Something to Wine About®."

It is absolutely amazing to me how I have been able to take my love of wine and people and create work that I truly love. It has taken me six years, six "Vision Days" with my own life coaches, and lots of hard work to build my idea into a business, but it continues to grow. Recently I expanded my column to three magazines, my radio show has been picked up by a station in a larger market and my first book, *The Sipping Point,* was published in July 2008.

Initially, it was not easy to walk away from a great paycheck to start my business, and there have been days when I wondered what I was thinking. But most days I am thrilled to be The Wine Coach®. I could not have envisioned how my business would grow or evolve when I began this endeavor, but each year I love it even more. I have finally found a way to share my passions and my unique gifts with the world. Who knows where my journey will take me next year?

LAURIE FORSTER, The Wine Coach® creates unique corporate keynotes and workshops that deliver on her mission of demystifying wine, one glass at a time. Laurie has shown hundreds of groups that wine tastings are the new golf outing. Laurie wrote *The Sipping Point*, released in 2008 to rave reviews, hosts a weekly radio show and contributes regularly to magazines. Interested in Laurie speaking to your group or association? Visit www.TheWineCoach.com and sign up for her free wine newsletter.

An Angel of Strength

Rising from the depths of pain to blaze a new career path

VICKI IRVIN

I felt strong, like this was something I definitely could do. Just another one of life's challenges I could get through with flying colors.

The nurses had started medications to begin the labor process. They warned me that I would slowly feel contractions that would intensify over the next couple of hours. I could handle physical pain. It was the emotional pain I struggled to stay in control of.

I appeared to be doing incredibly well. My husband, Lloyd, and my in-laws were at my side. We were laughing and joking and sharing stories. But when the nurse entered the room, the conversation stopped. She strode over to my bed, pamphlets in hand, and sat beside me. "Sweetie, you have to make a decision. Do you want to hold your baby and spend time with him?" she asked. "We strongly encourage you to see him, as part of the healing and closure process."

At that moment, the pressure became so overwhelming that I thought I would die. I put my hands over my face and was racked with sobs. Holding my baby suddenly seemed beyond my capacity. I didn't want images that would haunt me for the rest of my life.

The nurse patted my leg. She left literature to help me decide. I took a deep breath. Someone—I can't remember who—started talking again. The awkward moment was gone. We pretended it never happened.

This nightmare had begun during my eighth month of pregnancy. The doctors discovered that my son had Trisomy 13, a genetic disorder that typically results in the baby's death in the womb. There would be deformities. I spent the next weeks waiting for the child I was carrying to die.

The day finally came when the doctor could no longer detect the heartbeat. It was time to induce labor.

After I gave birth to my son, I held him for hours. I thought it was just minutes, unaware that the pain medication had made me lose all sense of time. But I did it. I had survived the loss of my first child.

As the nurse's assistant wheeled me out of the hospital, I kept my eyes down. I felt ashamed. I'm not sure why, for I had done nothing wrong.

I saw a family entering the delivery room, about five of them, walking quickly and looking very excited. The mother-to-be was in the center of the group, holding her stomach. I tensed up and felt my mother-in-law, my support system, do the same. I braced for the obvious question: "What did you have?" I found my inner strength and smiled weakly. "A boy." It took everything I had to utter those two words. They smiled back as they rushed past. "Congratulations!"

But they didn't know that my baby boy was stillborn.

I was wheeled out of the hospital and taken home, empty-handed, to resume my life.

GETTING ON WITH LIFE

Everyone handles grief differently. I resumed work, as a human resources professional, about a week and a half after delivering my son. I thought that getting back out there and facing the world was the best thing for me. There was no sense in hiding. I desperately wanted to have some normalcy back in my life.

Family and friends thought I was rushing things, merely pretending all was fine. But I really was OK, at least for the most part, until I developed a fear of being alone in the dark. Nighttime was scary for me, and I remember not wanting my husband to leave the house. It doesn't make sense to me why that happened, but it did. Still, I pushed all my fears aside with a determination I had never felt before.

After doing research on birth defects, I realized that I was just a statistic. We all know someone who had a miscarriage or lost a baby, but nobody imagines it will ever happen to them. It helped me immensely to understand that these things just happen, and I was just one of the people it happened to. Rather than blaming anyone, feeling sorry for myself or questioning God, I accepted what happened for what it was: one of those things in life you have no control over.

I joined forums and an organization of women who had been through similar experiences. Many were so devastated by the loss of a child that they gave up trying to get pregnant again. I understand feeling that way, but I would encourage them to realize that the odds of the same thing happening again are very small. The reward of having a child, to me, outweighs the risks.

With that positive attitude, I got pregnant again about six months later. Throughout my second pregnancy, the doctors monitored me closely. They required me to undergo genetic counseling and gave me my options on which tests I could take to determine if my baby had genetic problems. I decided against such invasive tests as amniocentesis because they pose a risk to the baby. Instead, I held onto reality and the fact that my prior pregnancy problems were a fluke. The chances of it happening again were slim to none. I wasn't afraid. I just knew that the baby I was carrying was healthy. I had another son who is the love of my life.

Everything in life happens for a reason, even if, at the time, we can't fathom what that reason is. It may be years before we figure it out, but there is a method to all of the madness. I am a firm believer that we cannot allow bad past experiences to cripple us or stop future happiness. It is a natural, human emotion to protect ourselves against pain. When we are hurt in a relationship or when we fail at a career, we tend to want to then play it safe. But playing it safe keeps us stuck in a place we don't want to be. We think we are doing the right thing, but we are actually stifling desires and dreams. Then you look up one day and realize your life has passed by, and you never got to do what you really wanted to do. This builds and harbors resentment.

I learned to conquer my fears so I would never have to look back and say that I regretted not pursuing what might have made me happy. Having a child with my husband was something I wanted very much. I refused to allow the fear and pain of what happened to my first baby to stop me—stop us—from experiencing that joy.

OTHER LIFE CHALLENGES

From my difficult experience, I now know that I can face, endure and do anything I want to do. I was a human resources professional, as I had been the majority of my career. I knew there was something else I wanted to do, but I didn't know what it was. I challenged myself to think hard about what I want to do professionally.

Lloyd was in his own world, buried in books, newsletters and studies with his mentors, Dan Kennedy and Bill Glazer, who help and encourage entrepreneurs with advertising and marketing strategies. Lloyd was constantly ranting and raving about marketing and running to the mailbox to get whatever latest informational newsletter he subscribed to. I thought my husband had lost his mind, as he seemed to be in a trance, on a mission to implement every money-making strategy he learned. And he *was* making lots of money. I saw him launch products online and make hundreds of thousands of dollars, sometimes in a day. There must be something to what he was doing.

As his guest, I attended a meeting of a mastermind group, a brainstorming and support group for businesspeople based on concepts introduced by Napoleon Hill in *Think and Grow Rich*. My eyes were opened to a brand new world. I was inspired by others who had started businesses from scratch or improved failing businesses following proven systems and models. It was the moment I had been waiting for. I knew this meeting would somehow be the catalyst for change in my career. I felt stronger than ever and determined to walk away with an idea or plan. I was ready to do something big.

At dinner with the mastermind team, I seized my moment. I told one of my husband's mentors, Bill Glazer, that I wanted to do something new. I suggested a couple of ideas, but he had something different in mind. We talked about the "pillars of wealth" and where the money was. Bill suggested I learn real estate investing. It was something I had always wanted to do, and I left the meeting determined to do just that.

But I went about the transition in the wrong way. After doing research on the Internet and watching late-night infomercials, I began ordering real estate investment CDs and tapes. Although I was excited, I quickly realized that real estate investing couldn't be learned like that. I felt discouraged, but I was on a mission. I was still strong, empowered and ready for anything. After expressing my frustrations to my husband, he introduced me to Terry Bryan, a colleague who is a successful real estate investor in Colorado. Terry took me under his wing and mentored me toward success, showing me what to do and how to do it.

CROWNING THE QUEEN

After becoming successful as an investor, I didn't want to stop there. The sky was the limit. Soon after learning real estate investing, I quit my job, what I liked to call "firing my boss." I decided to teach other people in my community in Prince George's County, Md., how to invest in real estate. No one else was doing it in a way that could reach people at all levels.

I became "The Real Estate Investment Queen." I enlisted the help of Lloyd and Terry Bryan, and we created Maryland Real Estate Secrets, the largest real estate investment program in the area. We teach 60 to 80 people each month how to invest in real estate and increase their wealth. Since the inception of the program, countless lives have been changed as a result of the education we share. With real estate investing, people acquire wealth so that they can do the things in life they want to do.

I always wondered what I could do in life to help affect others and promote positive change, but I never imagined it would be through real estate investing. I receive emails daily from people telling me how I motivate and inspire them, and thanking me for what I am doing in the community. That is one of the most rewarding things ever: helping other people to realize their dreams.

Time stops for no one. You can have all the money in the world, and if you lose the money, you can get it back. But you can never get back time. Once it's gone, it's gone. Our lives are precious, and how we spend our time is critical. Nobody else is responsible for our happiness, and anything worth having is going to take hard work.

I made a choice. I could have spent years complaining about working a traditional 9-5 job that left me restless and unfulfilled and do nothing about it. Or I could jump out there on faith, secure in my abilities and knowing that I can and will accomplish all that I set out to do. If I wasn't willing to work hard, then I shouldn't be complaining.

This doesn't mean I didn't have to battle fear, because I did. We are often taught to play everything safe. Many follow the basic patterns of going to college and getting a job. We are supposed to get married and have children. If we begin to have desires that take us away from this pattern that society follows, we become afraid. Afraid to break out of tradition and do something different, something risky. The fear of failure and hearing people say "I told you so" is strong, so strong that it keeps many people stuck. I have missed several opportunities in life out of fear. I regret them, but knowing that I finally found the guts and fortitude to battle fear and actually conquer it has made it OK.

Life is full of challenges. What makes us a winner is being able to handle those challenges when they are thrown our way. Everything is not always going to go according to our plans. Learning from each experience, whether it is good or bad, is what matters most. In fact, the lessons learned from painful experiences are sometimes the most important lessons. Adversity makes you stronger and more aware.

Surrounding yourself with positive people who help push you is also critical for achieving your dreams. In life you will meet many people who you initially consider friends, but who your true friends are is determined by who is still in your corner after you experience both failure and success. Those left standing beside you should be cherished.

I have pictures of my son who died. The hospital staff dressed him and took photographs because they knew it was part of the healing process. They also made impressions of his footprints. Every once in a while, when I'm feeling down or need to be reminded of my purpose or just need some extra strength, I take out those pictures and study them.

They remind me that nothing in life is guaranteed but that I can overcome anything that is thrown my way. They also are a reminder that no matter how hard I try, I cannot control everything, and that God has ultimate authority. But most of all they are a reminder that I have my

own personal angel looking down over me every single day. And for that I am grateful.

VICKI IRVIN, "The Real Estate Investment Queen," is a full-time real estate investor and coach in Prince George's County, Md. Along with her husband, Lloyd, she owns and operates Maryland Real Estate Secrets, one of the largest and most successful real estate investment groups in the Washington, D.C., metropolitan area. Vicki also owns www.Superwomanlifestyle.com, a business coaching practice for women. She enjoys working out, running, writing and inspiring others to follow their dreams.

The Courage to Be Who You Are

A long road to authenticity, identity and consciousness

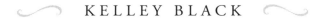 KELLEY BLACK

"Your job in this life is to have the courage to be yourself; to bow before no one but the God that sits in your heart." —Gurunam

Today as I strolled through the streets of the East Village in New York City, I reflected upon the business lunch I just left. One of my business partners paid me the highest compliment anyone had ever given me—and it had nothing to do with all that I've achieved. As we concluded lunch, he looked me dead in the eye and said, "You are a gift from God."

When I was very young, I innately knew this. I thought I was special. My parents were different: one was white and one was black. I had very curly, unruly hair, and no one seemed to know what to do with it. I defied definition. Some thought I was Israeli, others Latina, still others Brazilian—everything but what I actually was, which I found comical. Were they so narrow-minded that they couldn't see that I was the descendant of slaves, sharecroppers and illiterate French fur trappers?

To top it off, I was willful beyond belief, sometimes much to the chagrin of the adults around me. Still and all, I spent my days very happy with what I saw on the outside and how I felt on the inside. I felt like a queen—later affirmed at Montessori preschool, where I would sit on my "princess" chair and ask the other kids to wait on me. They willingly did, and everything seemed just fine.

DISCOVERING SHAME

What I didn't pick up on was that the reason no one had a clue as to what I was (remember, this was the 1970s) was that no one looked like me at all. And most didn't act like me either. I was the girl who defied Catholic school convention on picture day—the only day when we didn't have to wear uniforms. I proudly wore my Grr-animals pantsuit while the other girls sported frilly dresses and the boys wore navy blue suits. I felt proud to be different, uniquely me. That's why it was all so debilitating when I started to feel the opposite, when the same qualities that I had embraced and felt emboldened by suddenly became a source of shame.

Two incidents stand out in my mind that triggered a reversal of fortune and a lack of clear self-identity. This reversal would lead me through a good 25 years of overachieving to the point of mental and physical exhaustion; excessive people-pleasing; the general silencing of my voice, self-esteem and authenticity; the attempted assassination of my soul; and some pretty self-destructive behavior. When I say "self-destructive," I'm not referring to the obvious ways that come to mind, e.g., drugs, alcohol and sex. What I mean is the slow, insidious neglect of the soul's calling, the stifling of all that I knew to be true in order to "fit in."

The first incident was when my Aunt Anne, drunk, screamed at me, "You think you're better than everyone. You think you're white!" The other was when a male classmate kept pulling up the skirt of my Sacred Heart Catholic School uniform while calling me a "nigger." These two incidents were the beginning of a sort of negative racial consciousness that up to that point didn't register in my psyche. The truth was that I didn't really think of myself as white or black. Until I was seven years old, I thought of myself simply as human, exotic and wonderful.

Shortly after Auntie Dearest's tirade, a girlfriend told me that she couldn't come for a picnic with us because my father was "black." I told her she was stupid, but all the while I longed for her to come with us and somehow validate that my family was worthy. The message I got from the episode was that, to even begin to not be seen as "other," I would have to establish my worth through everyone else's eyes.

Simply being me was not enough. I would need to be prettier, more athletic, achieve better grades and most of all not show my feelings or who I really was. I began to construct a façade that I felt would get me out of that place to somewhere bigger than the small, Waspy New England college town I grew up in. I joined the swim team, took advanced placement classes, and began to over-identify with everyone else's needs.

At this point, my parents were divorced and my mom, younger sister and I rarely saw my dad. He became a sort of phantom myth—the man who had grown up poor and abused, who had put himself through college and grad-school on the GI bill, married my mother in defiance of the convention of the times and became a C-Level executive at Digital Equipment Corp. (He also had a substance abuse problem, abandoned us and was emotionally absent even when he was physically there.)

My survival instinct was to construct a myth to explain what was going on: My father wasn't in rehab; he was off being wealthy and fabulous (he was wealthy and fabulous until ego, excess and the demons of his past caught up with him). My mom wasn't emotionally unavailable; she was stoic, strong and principled (she was all of these things but under the pressure of being a single mom and her own grief she didn't have a lot of time for helping us process what was going on. Her cultural/ bloodline imprinting was "stiff upper lip" and keep moving). My sister wasn't suffering equally; she was just odd, introverted and competitive for the meager resources that were available to us. And we weren't struggling; we just liked to do "other things." For example, we weren't getting ice cream cones because we didn't like them, not because there wasn't the $2 needed to buy them.

Grandmother MeMe's lap was the one place where I felt unconditional love, where I could get the hugs, and empathy I needed (frequently aided by a mixed drink). MeMe always made me feel like I was more than good enough, and for this I am still grateful.

So while I was earning A's, winning state championships and setting records in swimming, plus achieving high scores on my SATs, I also was developing a severe eating disorder, which turned into full-blown anorexia and bulimia that lasted well into my 20s. We were struggling to pay the bills and, with my father paying child support sporadically and my mother working two jobs to pay the mortgage, there was not much emotional support. In fact, my sister and I really weren't allowed to "feel" anything.

The implicit message was that, if we expressed how we felt, bad things would happen. So we didn't. I turned all the anger, hurt, sadness and brokenness inward, and the overriding sense of always having to prove myself became dominant. The feeling of always being "alone," even when surrounded by other people, gnawed at my very soul. I was frozen.

Yes, I put up a good front. I made my way out of that small town, first to Princeton, N.J., and later to New York. While living in Princeton, I began my long walk back to myself. And, in retrospect, I believe God watched over me the whole time. By grace and good fortune, I became part of a wonderful family led by two exceptional people who to this day are wonderful global citizens. I found people who could, individually and in their marriage, mirror back to me complete, sometimes messy, but basically happy lives. I owe much to them because, simply out of the goodness of their hearts, they showed me unconditional love and introduced me to a worldview that was vast, colorful and limitless. And most of all, they validated me for exactly who I was, including the messy, indefinable bits. Plus, they introduced me to travel and very good wine!

A JOB FOR AN OVERACHIEVER

Moving to New York was the best thing I ever did. New York in many ways has been my primary relationship for the last 18 years. New York is like the lover that found my every weakness, revealed it to me, held me accountable and then presented me with the resources to dig my way out. This love/hate relationship has broken me more than once, but it also has presented me with the opportunity to heal and rebuild myself.

It was in New York that I found my first career: pharmaceutical advertising/marketing. This was my field for 12 good years, the exception being one miserable year spent in marketing at L'Oreal. Advertising is a great place for an overachiever. While I was in it, advertising was an industry that applauded excessive behavior. No one was going to tell me to slow down, take a vacation, and think about nurturing myself. But it was no one else's job to do that. It was mine, and I had no idea how to do it.

Everything looked good on paper. I was traveling the world, making a sizeable income, buying lots of designer shoes, climbing the corporate ladder, being applauded for my ability to charm clients and colleagues alike, and I had the blond bombshell boyfriend/fiancé on top of it. I should note that regarding this point, the boyfriend was far too stable, loving, practical and successful for me to accept him.

After the wedding invitations had been sent out and plans made, I freaked out and broke up with him. This is when I became really wayward. I was a workaholic with a revolving door of relationships. Oh yes, it was quite easy to attract boyfriends, but they were never the right ones and every year or two it was time for a replacement.

One day I woke up and couldn't get out of bed. I had a nervous breakdown. I tried to slit my wrists. I phoned my sister, Taunya, who put me on a train to Massachusetts, where my mother lived, and essentially saved my life. To this day, I believe that if it hadn't been for her I wouldn't have made it. From Massachusetts, I was sent to my father in Atlanta, where I spent day after day looking at the ceiling in my bedroom and thinking, "This cannot be happening."

But it was. I was on antidepressants and tried to commit suicide a second time by downing a bottle of pills. I was never hospitalized but saw a couple of shrinks; still, I found the whole thing to be a joke. The psychiatrists just kept prescribing pills and the psychologists kept revisiting my parents divorce and my biracial heritage; they just seemed to be always writing in a pad and saying, "Uh-huh," which made me want to SCREAM.

Eventually, I said to hell with all of them. And, weird as it may sound, I started to play tennis and to slowly come alive again. It was funny, but the only time I would get out of bed was to play tennis matches that my dad had arranged for me. It was such a dark time in my life that it temporarily forced me to start looking inside. I had lost the trappings of success and couldn't hide. I hadn't merely slowed down; my life as I knew it had imploded.

The problem was that I was still quite willful and, after three months, I told my dad that I was going back to New York. He later told me that he wept after he dropped me at the airport because I was so frail he thought I wouldn't survive.

Luckily, I was embraced by my industry when I returned. After all, I knew my stuff and I could still produce. I went back to my old career and my workaholic ways. I also became involved with a French rogue restaurant owner. You can just imagine how healthy that was!

I kept thinking that, if I just worked harder, made more money and lived more fabulously, somehow I would be accepted and acceptable. I vowed to rebuild my life. What I failed to realize is that I *was* accepted and acceptable. The external stuff was there, but I didn't listen to or respect myself. Still, I was trying to nurture my soul. I went to church on Sundays; I worked out, but nothing was integrated. I had no real relationship with my soul or with God. Faith, hope and love were in short supply.

And, just when I thought it was safe, life up-ended me yet again. There was a very big political shakeup at the ad agency I was working for, and I was called into the president's office and told that I was being fired because of inappropriate behavior on a photo shoot. It was an odd thing to be reprimanded for behavior that wasn't mine and that I had no control over. And it didn't even happen at the shoot; it happened hours later—when I was asleep. The whole notion that I was being fired because of someone else's behavior when I wasn't even present was so ludicrous that I started laughing and said, "You're kidding."

They weren't. The next thing I knew I was escorted to my desk to clean out my personal things and then I was physically walked out of the office. I experienced a whole range of emotions—indignation, disgust, betrayal, shock and anger. I also knew that I was completely burned out, physically, mentally and emotionally. This occurred two months after 9/11. I was dealing with survival issues on a number of levels.

Two days later, I was getting phone calls from other agencies and headhunters trying to recruit me. Some of them seemed absolutely gleeful at the prospect of getting me to come on board, and no one seemed the slightest bit fazed about what had gone down. In a volatile industry, the response was more to the effect that people couldn't believe that it had taken 12 years for me to get caught up in some shakeup. They thought I had a great run. I thought it was all very, very weird!

SETTING EVERYTHING RIGHT

So I just stopped. I stopped and began to take stock. I didn't take another job in the industry I knew so well and was a success in. I realized that I was over the whole thing and didn't want to do it anymore. The challenge was that I had no idea what to do next.

Here was the gift in all of it: I made it my primary goal to get healthy in a whole and integrated way and began to investigate ways of doing so. I started by going to Pilates school and training in classical Pilates. I had no intention of teaching, but I really wanted to understand how to stay healthy from a structural alignment standpoint.

Years of office work and many flights across time zones had left me with chronic shoulder and neck pain. Pilates got my body fit and strong and satisfied my intellect. The biomechanics, anatomy and physiology of the discipline were all very interesting. I had spent so much time in my head that it was fun to learn about my body and how to heal it on a deeper level.

I also was graced with meeting my teacher and mentor, Joseph Michael Levry (Gurunam). Gurunam means "he who leads them from darkness to light." This meeting proved to be the most auspicious event of my life, the catalyst to setting everything right.

In meeting Gurunam, I learned the art and science of Kundalini Yoga, NAAM Yoga and Universal Kabbalah. These spiritual teachings have been the great savior in my life. They provided me with the platform to obtain true self-healing by learning how to face and overcome my own darkness, clear negative self-limiting patterns, open my heart and have the courage to be exactly who I am. Studying with Gurunam enabled me to walk back to the young girl who knew she was special, who accepted herself as exactly who she was, who felt that she was a queen because she knew she was a gift from God, as we all are.

The process of self-healing bore beautiful fruits, and out of the ashes rose a phoenix. There is a favorite saying among Universal Kabbalists that you can tell the quality of the gold by the fire it has been through. Not too long ago, I jokingly asked Gurunam if I might qualify for platinum status.

I am grateful and thank God for every part of my journey. Each part, no matter how painful, has helped mold me into who I am today, and I would venture to say that it made me more compassionate and service-oriented than I would have been otherwise. I feel rich beyond measure. With the help of many, I am realizing my dream of changing the paradigm of stress management through the evolutionary self-healing techniques that benefited me so greatly.

My clients (executives who are determined to live a healthy lifestyle) tell me that my business, Balancing the Executive Life, has changed their lives. My husband, Andrew Zelmer, blesses me daily with his unconditional love. My sister Taunya and my niece Ameena fill my life with more grace than words can express. I am surrounded by incredible people in my business and personal lives. I am healthy in mind, body and spirit. My cup runneth over with love, faith and hope, and I know anything is possible.

KELLEY BLACK lives in New York City where she founded and created the well-known and acclaimed program Balancing The Executive Life™ to prevent business leaders from suffering illness and burn-out. After 12 years of corporate experience, she took a sabbatical to pursue her own healing, gaining extensive knowledge of self-healing, energetic laws and resilience strategies. To learn more about her corporate programs, contact her at Kelley@balancingexec.com or go to website www.balancingexec.com.

From Volunteer to CEO

How a family tragedy set me on a course of public service

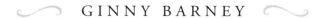 GINNY BARNEY

It was a typical snowy Saturday morning in February. Inside our warm, snug home, the kids' Valentine's Day decorations were still taped to the refrigerator door. My husband, Marshall, had gone to the office to catch up on some work. The kids and I were lounging in our pajamas. I was reading the paper. My 5-year-old daughter, Joy, was watching cartoons, and my 2-year-old son, Brad, was playing with his trucks. Every few minutes he would jump up, dash to another room, grab a different toy and then race back. It was just an ordinary Saturday morning in Upper Arlington, a suburb of Columbus, Ohio.

Suddenly I heard a loud pop and Brad's scream. I jumped up and ran to the other room, where I saw Brad racing toward me screaming and a wall of flames behind him. He had poked something into an electrical socket, which sparked and set the floor-to-ceiling drapes on fire. I grabbed him, ran for the fire extinguisher on the basement stairs and screeched to a halt. With Brad in my arms and Joy now joining in the terror, there was no way I could put out the fire. I didn't even know how to operate the fire extinguisher. I ran to the kitchen phone, but couldn't remember the number of the fire department (there was no 9-1-1 in 1980). I dialed my husband's office in a panic and, thankfully, someone there called the fire department. I grabbed coats to wrap around the kids and ran outside. We stood in the snow, still wearing pajamas and fuzzy slippers.

Mere minutes seemed like forever as we waited. Finally, we heard the sirens growing louder and the fire trucks arrived. The firefighters rushed into the house, and the medics ushered us into the emergency squad vehicle. One of the medics said we needed to transport Brad to the hospital. I asked if I could go in the house to grab some clothes. He said, "Lady, you aren't going back in there for several hours." Another medic radioed Children's Hospital that they were en route with a toddler with burns over 18 percent of his body. Reality set in and a deep sense of loss invaded my body and mind—loss of safety, loss of security and loss of control.

LIFE IN TURMOIL

Brad was admitted to the restricted Firefighter's Burn Unit due to the high risk of infection. Only immediate family could visit and then for only a few hours at a time. Brad's hands and legs were bandaged. We would rock him, and read or sing to him. We tried to feed him, but he was in pain and exhausted. When we had to leave the unit, he looked terrified. I felt utterly helpless.

In the house, fire damaged only one room, but smoke ruined the entire structure. Every rug, every drape, every wall, every piece of clothing smelled. Smoke invaded every piece of food, including cereal that was still sealed from the store. It crept inside all the glasses turned upside down in closed cupboards.

Joy, Marshall and I moved into a hotel, and my mother rushed to join us. She drove 10 straight hours and arrived by nightfall. For days, she took care of all of us. We were exhausted, frazzled and numb from the ordeal.

Just as the smoke from the fire had invaded everything in our house, I realized that it had just as pervasively intruded upon my thoughts. I couldn't close my eyes without the vision of Brad with the flames behind him. The first night, I tried to read myself to sleep. Every time I nodded off, I would jerk awake, terrified, reliving the day. I finally slipped out of the room and walked the halls of the hotel until morning. After three sleepless nights, I went to the doctor for sleeping pills. The flashbacks slowly disappeared.

The knot in my stomach took longer to leave. I knew I needed to keep up my strength for all that needed to be done, but I just couldn't force the food down. I lost 10 pounds the first week, and it continued from there. Eventually, logic stepped in and, little by little, bite by bite, I regained my appetite.

When we weren't visiting with Brad in the hospital, we were getting the house back in order. We wanted to be back in our home before Brad was released. Carpets were ripped out, walls painted, food thrown out, dishes and clothes washed. The amount of work was overwhelming, but the response from our neighbors and friends was astonishing. People wanted to help, and we needed them. Some brought food, some took loads of laundry home to wash and return, and some babysat Joy. One family even offered their house to us when they went on vacation.

After 14 days in the burn unit, we brought our little boy home. As Brad's burns healed, we continued to deal with the psychological effects of the fire. Every night, Brad had nightmares in which he fought the fire. During the day, everyone had to get comfortable again being around backyard grills, fireplaces, birthday candles, sirens and even doctors. We visited the fire station a lot and volunteered to raise money for the burn unit. Fire safety became our family mission.

REGAINING CONTROL

I asked the Upper Arlington Fire Division to help us raise money for the Children's Hospital Firefighter Burn Unit. In exchange, they asked me to volunteer to teach fire safety in the schools. In a moment of agreeing, my life of public service began.

I recruited two friends and together we researched educational materials, met with school principals, and scheduled presentations to every class—preschool through eighth grade—in the city. We wore red jackets with the city fire logo on them and carried photo identification. It was 1981, and we were the only comprehensive, age-appropriate fire-safety education program in the area. We were volunteers, but we were experts. I taught firefighters from other areas how to start their own programs. I even did a couple workshops through the state fire marshal's office sharing a victim's perspective for hospital and fire emergency personnel. That's how the Fire Safety Education Program in Upper Arlington began. I'm proud to say that it continues today with a paid staff.

That volunteer experience enabled me to meet my fears, share my knowledge, and feel like I was doing something important in my community. It felt good to be giving children and their parents tools to prevent a fire or information on what to do if, heaven forbid, they were in a fire. With each class I taught, my sense of safety and security slowly returned. Knowledge gave me back my sense of control.

BECOMING A PUBLIC SERVANT

Five years later, I was asked to lead the efforts for a police and fire pension levy. I agreed; it was a natural extension of my volunteer service. Two years later, when there was an opening on city council, I was asked to apply for an appointment. Of the 17 people who applied, I was chosen to fill the unexpired term. I was subsequently elected to two four-year terms on council, including serving as vice mayor and then mayor. In Upper Arlington, there is a city manager form of government. My leadership roles on council were to preside at the council meetings and to perform ceremonial jobs. I was on the policy side of government.

To this day, I'm not sure I would ever have run for city council if I hadn't been appointed first. It feels much more comfortable for me to be asked to do something rather than to launch a campaign stating that I was the best person for the job. It takes a lot of courage to stand forward, sharing your opinions, and asking for people's financial support and, ultimately, their votes. Politicians do it everyday, but it was not my style.

In public office, my business training gave me the skills to quickly understand the financial and operational side of running a city. My passion for children and interest in safety served me well on the programmatic side. I loved it. I was serving my community, working with great staff and helping people.

However, I quickly learned that, in some people's eyes, I had turned from a wonderful community volunteer to a no-good politician. The same people who had given me accolades and awards were wondering

what my motives might be. I was not prepared for that. People who had called me "Ginny" for years started to call me "Virginia"—the name used on the ballot and in the media. I called "Virginia" my stage name. (I'm now equally comfortable with either name.)

After one particularly heated community discussion, I called a friend—the room mother in my son's fourth-grade class—who was on the other side of the issue from my vote. She was so angry that she said she couldn't talk to me and hung up. I remember climbing in the shower and crying, wondering what I had gotten myself into. I grew up quickly.

Many, many friends and residents did write to tell me how much they appreciated my community service, but the ones who didn't like what I was doing seemed to write letters to the editor for the whole world to see. That was tough, particularly for my family. I saved the letters of support and appreciation and threw away the ones that were not so kind. I knew that I would need to reread the positive notes when times got rough and that I would remember the negative notes without even looking at them. I developed a thick skin, but have tried to keep my heart soft.

In May 1998, the Republican Party asked me to run for an appointment to the Franklin County Clerk of Courts. In Ohio, the county clerk supports the common pleas court and the district court of appeals as well as running the auto title offices for the county. It is an operation with multiple offices, more than 200 employees, and well in excess of $225 million is collected each year.

The previous clerk had just pled guilty to charges of theft in office of about $500,000 and was sentenced to six years in prison. The office was in chaos, the employees all under suspicion, and the likely opponent in the upcoming election was from a third-generation political family with big name recognition. I'm sure other possible candidates were approached to throw a hat in the ring, and they ran screaming in the other direction. For all intents and purposes, this looked like a lose-lose scenario.

GREATER RESPONSIBILITY

To me, it looked like an opportunity to use my gifts, make a difference and to help the employees find the right course for the office. After being interviewed, I was appointed as the first woman Clerk of Franklin County.

The first few days in the office of clerk, I met with the county prosecutor, representatives of the state auditor's office, and officers of the state Bureau of Criminal Investigation. I learned how the theft was committed, how long it had likely been going on, who might have known about the crime, and where the hidden cameras were in my office. At the end of the first week, I fired the top four people in leadership roles. If they didn't know about the crime, they should have. We needed a whole new team to rebuild the public's trust in our office.

I had an open-door policy for any employee with a complaint, a suggestion or a story to tell. I heard plenty of stories: about sex acts on my desk (I scrubbed everything down after that conversation!); about raises given for political campaign support; about racial discrimination; about lack of financial controls; about inconsistent personnel rules; and about a lack of training opportunities. The office was a mess.

Clearly, I needed help. From my years of volunteering in the community, I knew volunteers sharing their talents could quickly make a huge difference. People were eager to help. From across political party lines, I formed a blue-ribbon task force of experts. It included a CFO of a national bank and the managing partner of a large accounting firm to help with financial controls and money management, a vice president of personnel for a national insurance company to work on personnel policies, a CEO of a public relations firm to help inform the public of how our office works, and many other volunteers who cared about good government. These task force members became our unpaid consultants and shared their gifts and knowledge freely.

The employees worked together to write a code of ethics for the office. All of us received ethics training and were trained on new financial policies. Everything was designed and implemented to give the public confidence that we protected the public's money and deserved their trust. Shortly after my appointment, I had to campaign for the office I was holding. I won re-election handily! My hard work, along with that of the employees and the volunteers, paid off. It felt great.

Two years later, the clerk's office was running smoothly, and the employees were well trained and proud. Written policies and procedures

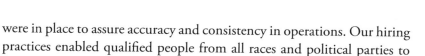

were in place to assure accuracy and consistency in operations. Our hiring practices enabled qualified people from all races and political parties to obtain jobs in our office.

Elected office can be very seductive, and it's very dangerous to start believing your own press releases. People started planning my future for me. I could be the next county commissioner, I was told, or the next member of Congress or the next state treasurer. It was amazing. In my heart, I wasn't so sure, but I knew I would recognize the right opportunity when it appeared.

When I got a call to return to the City of Upper Arlington as its city manager or CEO, I listened carefully. I loved restoring the public's trust in the clerk's office, meeting the challenge of organizing the office and empowering the employees. Taking the nonpartisan city manager position would disappoint all those folks who were planning my future, but I was unhappy and uncomfortable in the bickering political party environment outside the office.

DECISION-MAKING STRATEGY

After considering all the advice, I needed to listen to my own voice. What was best for me? I asked myself three questions to help make my decision. It is the same strategy I use today before taking on any new commitment, even if it's a volunteer position.

1. **Will it use my gifts?** We all have talents and skills. If I'm working and using mine, I'm happy and productive.
2. **Can I make a difference?** Even if I'm using my talents, I might not be able to move the organization along. If I'm not the right fit for the organization, it's not the right fit for me.
3. **Will it be fun?** Sure, there are difficult days in any job, but life should be enjoyable. If I dread going to work everyday, I'm not doing my best, and I'm not in the right place.

In considering the city manager position, the answer to all three questions was yes! The variety of talents in a city organization is energizing. Where else can I have engineers, CPAs, attorneys, fire and police chiefs, park and recreation experts, architects and more in the same room working on the same goal of a better community?

In my experience in private business, everyone guards trade secrets and shares nothing. In public service, there are no secrets. Everyone shares their best practices as well as their problems freely so all can learn to serve better. It's a wonderful, giving environment where I thrive and have fun.

Working in a city enables me to meet with school kids and senior citizens daily. I have the opportunity to impact their lives. Through community committees and projects, I get to know what people care about, and we work together to help them enjoy the services and community they want. Upper Arlington is a city of about 34,000 residents. It's large enough to provide significant programs and projects and small enough to see them come to life. Public service is tremendously satisfying for me.

I have a weekly city manager column in our local newspaper, attempting to put a face on government as I share items of interest or importance with our residents. Over the years, people have come to recognize me. They stop me in the grocery store and share a concern or thank me for a particular service they received. For the most part, I really enjoy talking with them. There are moments when a little anonymity would be helpful, like the time I was buying a bra and panties at Macy's and the man behind me in line chose to make my acquaintance at that very moment!

My job as a public servant is to help elected leaders and our residents create a place where families can raise their children, where people can grow old and still stay connected, where people feel safe, where there are opportunities to play and enjoy nature in our parks, where we can shop and work. My job is to help people build a community.

When a house fire led me to my volunteer career as a fire-safety educator, I had no idea I would hold elected office and eventually return to Upper Arlington as the CEO of the city. In my mind, there's no job more fulfilling. I leave my office every day feeling that I have touched someone's life. It's a responsibility I don't take lightly and a privilege I don't take for granted.

I am happy to report my son Brad is married, perfectly healthy and recently celebrated his 31st birthday. He has forgotten the events surrounding our house fire. What he remembers is attending my fire safety classes.

VIRGINIA BARNEY lives with Marshall, her husband of 39 years, in Upper Arlington, a suburb of Columbus, Ohio. Their grown children, Brad and Joy, are out of the house, but live close by. Virginia has served as the city manager since 2000. She sits on numerous community boards and continues to advocate for fire safety education. She shares her story in the hopes that others will consider public service as a place to share their talents.

Finding Love
Way Past 40

Wait until the time is right, then get out of the way

M . E .   J O N E S

"You not married?" my boss's Korean assistant asked me. "What wrong with you?" I laughed at first. Her bluntness was funny, but later I was highly offended.

There seems to be a collective unconsciousness that believes that, no matter how successful a woman is, if she doesn't have a man in her life, all of her accomplishments are diminished. Some people just hint at it, but others can't stop themselves from stating it pointedly.

As a single woman, I've dealt with this attitude most of my adult life.

At some point, I gave up on love. And so have most of my female friends. Sometimes one of us would find love by fluke. A professor friend said, "The only way I'm going to meet a man is if he literally knocks on my door." And that's just what happened—she married the cable guy!

More common were the countless dateless Friday nights that we women—accomplished, beautiful, smart, funny women—would go to dinner, complaining that there were no available men. They were all married, gay or just not that into us.

But eventually I stopped commiserating with my friends. It had started to get depressing, and it just wasn't me. I made a pact with myself that if I wasn't willing to fix something in my life, I had to stop complaining about it.

YOUNG LOVE

When I was 16, I fell in love. I'll call the object of my affection James. James lived in Washington, D.C., where I spent my summers. Our connection was instant and intense. I tried to be cool, but there just wasn't enough time, as it was already August when we met. He was so sure of me that it was intoxicating. We spent so much time together that his mother asked to meet me. Apparently, I was keeping James from his tennis practice. After the summer break, I returned to California, a lovesick high school freshman.

For two years, James wrote me love letters a couple times a week. Quietly but consistently, he set a standard for the level of devotion, respect and intimacy I would come to expect from men. At 17, he was exceptional in expressing his feelings. Our relationship cooled when he chose Harvard over Stanford at the last minute, ruining our plans to at least be on the same coast. I was heartbroken.

Little did I know it would take another 33 years to attract this same kind of love.

I remember it being easy to connect with men and start a relationship. But as infatuation wore off and our real personalities showed up, of course we broke up. I survived two major relationships in my 20s and another two in my 30s. Twice I even felt married—and both of these men refer to me as their ex-wife. Not knowing what was to come, I felt lucky to have loved and been loved by these men, even the closet alcoholic, pothead jerk (enough said on that matter!). Each time, I didn't think I would recover. But I did.

In 1978, a boyfriend wanted to get married and move to Iran. Why didn't I know this before we got serious? Yes, I saw the movie *Not Without My Daughter* starring Sally Field. Everyone told me, "That could have been you, M.E.!" Another boyfriend wanted me to get pregnant, and *then* he would marry me and we'd live happily ever after. What? What kind of backward, forced hand was this? Then there was Mr. Perpetual Peter Pan, whom I lived with for almost five years. My older sister reminds me, "He robbed you of your child-bearing years!"

DIVING INTO CAREER

I continued to leap in without reservations, but I was missing something—a soul connection, a spiritual connection. I thought I had commitment issues for a long time, but in reality, I just wasn't with the right man.

When I was 36, the pressure to find a man at any cost grew tiring. It was coming at me from all angles, and I had to fend it off. So I retreated into myself. I over-ate and over-exercised, but mostly I over-achieved. My plan was to forge full steam ahead on my career, which fulfilled me… until it didn't anymore.

For more than 20 years I worked in the entertainment industry. My first job was as an audience page for a television studio. Next I worked in payroll and in client services, then as a production manager, an associate producer and eventually producer. The last 10 years, I produced sitcoms for various networks and studios. The physical work of putting on a show was challenging and fun. It was my job to manage the production, the budget, the crew and staff.

The "people" work was emotionally and physically draining. I felt like a mother to some very bad children, only these were highly paid adults. I burned out on all the dysfunctional behavior. Sexual harassment, drinking and drugging at work, gambling (yes, people called their bookies from the stage), nepotism (continues to this day), discrimination (all kinds), foul language, and emotional and physical abuse were rampant. It's amazing that anything got done.

I sat in on casting sessions with predominately male writers and producers to lend a female voice in the room. The comments these men made after an actress left the room were horrifying. They would let loose about her looks (or lack thereof), her marital status, her dating practices, clothes, mother, and on and on. Little would be said about her acting ability. I kept thinking, "Surely they've forgotten I'm in the room!" But they just didn't care. I have to admit I was not happy with men during this time. When I got home at night, the last thing I wanted to do was date them.

TAKING A DEEPER LOOK

My anger showed itself in the form of debilitating lower back pain. I knew I had some unresolved emotional issues. My father passed away the year before, and I hadn't grieved fully. I remember bursting out crying when I saw a bride being walked down the aisle by her father on a soap opera. I never fantasized about this, but seeing this image ignited something in me.

A friend recommended the book *Getting To I Do* by Dr. Patricia Allen, saying it had helped her understand and appreciate men. The book points out all the mistakes women make with men simply because they speak a different language.

To work on the disappointment I felt with men, as the book suggested, I tried to define what kind of woman I was. Did I possess more feminine or masculine traits? And what kind of man did I want to attract? I had to really think about this. It took a long time for me to grasp this concept of masculine and feminine men and how it affects the roles in a relationship.

In the process, I kept thinking about the man instead of about me. I remember throwing Dr. Allen's book across the room a couple of times. I resisted change. But what I realized was that I didn't need to change who I was, just my behavior, which was inconsistent with what I said I wanted. Eventually, the method did work, and I started appreciating men again. The lessons I learned from the book were powerful and life changing.

Had I forgotten that my own mother was a strong, feminine, independent, smart, funny, stay-at-home mom? She and my dad had a very interdependent relationship with clearly defined roles. I always felt that my mother was an equal partner with my dad, always. My mom eventually returned to work and college (at age 65) and graduated with honors.

After observing my relationship struggles, my mother shared with me that she had chosen to marry again after her first husband died suddenly, leaving her with a six-month-old baby. She bought their house with the life insurance settlement and tried to love again. The next time around, it lasted almost 53 years. So I had good role models for a productive, long marriage.

"You want to be married and single at the same time," Mom told me. She was right. I wanted the good stuff and none of the bad, especially not someone telling me what to do. I did have a major problem with that. She also reminded me, "You don't have to react to everything men say. Didn't you notice that I ignored about 50 percent of what your father says?" Wow, that was a lot, considering he was the strong, silent type.

IS WANTING A WEAKNESS?

At this point, I was 48 years old, very single and even somewhat reclusive. I bought into the myth that attracting love or marriage was impossible at that age. I did some serious praying and meditating just to cancel out this thinking. There is this "thing" that happens to successful, independent and self-sufficient women. It happened to me. I became embarrassed to want a man—like it was beneath me to want to fall in love and have someone cherish, marry and actually support me. My ego told me this was a weakness for a highly accomplished woman. Digging down really deep, I asked myself this question: "Do you really want to be alone for the second half of your life?" I cried about it. I was pissed off (again, it felt weak!). I was stubborn and indignant, but I kept asking.

Then it happened.

I found love.

Trust me ladies, love can be had in your 40s, 50s, 60s and beyond. I am living proof.

What did I do? I finally treated my love life as if it were one of my career goals and attacked it with the same focus and energy. And yes, it took that same intention and passion I had once had for producing television shows.

I looked at my situation logically. I needed to have a pool of available, relationship-ready men. Not an introduction here, a set-up there, or a dinner party where he and I are the only single people invited. I needed volume so I could reject or accept men on my terms. No more hits or misses. Where could I put myself in a situation where there are a lot of available men?

I joined an online relationship site matching singles based on compatibility.

I took a test and realized I hadn't thought about what I really wanted in a man in a long time. I hadn't done the prep work, so I was willing to talk to anyone who showed some interest. The test on the website was more than 400 questions and took me almost two hours to complete. Plus, I needed to include my profile and other preferences. After finishing up, something shifted in me. I felt in control, motivated, and sort of excited.

Why this time? I have no idea. I just knew I was ready to give my love life the focus it needed. I knew intuitively I was going to meet my partner. I knew because I made it a goal. I was no longer embarrassed. My focus and determination were just like going after any other goals, ones I had set and achieved. But most important, I finally knew what I wanted in a man.

THE WEEDING PROCESS

I was methodical, unemotional and relentless. I would check the website early in the morning for new matches and start communicating. Then I'd go back online in the evening, advancing to the next step. I did have a few meltdowns, but I talked myself through them. I weeded and weeded through a couple hundred men. Where else would I have the opportunity to meet 200 men over the course of a couple of months?

At times it felt like a job. I had to be organized and present. Most of my matches were not in California. The few matches I had in my area closed me out because I did not post my photo. At first the rejection was startling, but some men wanted to see me first before they invested any time getting to know me. I understood this.

Then there were some, like me, who wanted to start from the inside.

MR. RIGHT

One of my first matches was a man living in Michigan. Once we got past all the formalities and started emailing, our online conversations began to gel. His questions and answers were thoughtful and intelligent. We shared a love of nature, politics, sports and writing. Rich made it clear from the onset that he wasn't looking for just a friend. Neither was I. Done.

Then we shared photos. Great! He's cute. And he thinks I'm cute. That was out of the way.

Then we started sharing more details of our lives. I wrote my abbreviated life story for him, and he described his life in a small rural town near Lake Huron. This went on for a week or two. I was still pursuing other matches, but I kept coming back to Rich. Love shows up in strange ways, I knew, but a farmer in rural Michigan?

We emailed each other about everything. Serious, silly, painful—life stuff. Rich wrote about communing with nature during his daily walks with Bootsie, his "borrowed" dog. He was continuing his father's legacy by serving his community in the health care field. I loved this about him.

He gave me his phone number and left it up to me to call when I felt comfortable. I resisted. Once again, my pride almost won out. But one Saturday morning, Nov. 20, 2005, to be exact, with heart palpitations, I called him.

That call changed my life.

Rich was friendly, upbeat and casual. Our conversation was unforced and lovely. We hung up after 10 minutes, and that was just enough—a "nibble" of Rich.

We talked sporadically over the next few weeks, then daily. We met, after much discussion, on his turf in January 2006. I mustered up the courage to go, but had a back-up plan and a girlfriend to call (with a secret word) in case he was a serial killer. Thankfully, none of that was needed.

Rich met me at the security gate. I was so nervous and excited that I hung back and was the last person off the plane. Very tentatively, I walked up the jet way toward him and called his name. I glimpsed into his beautiful blue eyes for the first time.

Shy at first, we hugged and kissed. We were strangers who knew each other's hearts.

At lunch and during the three-hour drive to his hometown, the reality of being physically together slowly started to catch up with the emotional connection we had made long distance over the past months.

Then, everything magically seemed to fall into place.

Three years later, I am fully committed to a man who loves me the way I have been waiting to be loved since my Harvard man in 10th grade. I did the work. I broke through my patterns and negativities. I expected to find love, be cherished, respected and accepted and—guess what?—I am. And I accept him in all of his "gentleman farmer" glory.

Rich is mature, stable and masculine, and we have a deep level of consciousness with one another. Our values are similar, as both of our parents were loving and supportive. He gets it that I flip-flop between my masculine and feminine selves, and he loves it. He gives me gentle reminders about my tone, and I know exactly what that means—my "boss voice" has entered the room. There is no drama in this relationship. We work through our differences, and so far have come out better on the other side. I feel supported in my dreams. He tells me his life is better with me in it, and I feel the same. We have great chemistry in every way.

On New Year's Eve, Rich and I were apart, and I was watching the movie *Shall We Dance,* with Richard Gere and Susan Sarandon. In the movie, Susan's character suspects her husband is cheating on her and hires a detective, only to find out he's taking ballroom dancing. When the detective asks her, "Why did you get married?" She says, "Because I want a witness for my life." I understood what she meant. Rich is my witness, and I am his.

WHERE WE ARE NOW

After more than two years of daily phone calls, trips, cards and flowers, I made the leap and moved to Michigan in August of 2008. Our plan is to eventually live in Michigan for eight months and California for four months (or some other warm place).

Moving across the country and adjusting to a live-in partner has been stressful at times. I am not only living in Rich's space and enduring a very long winter, I am dealing with what I call "farm issues." Specifically, Farmer Rich vs. The Weasel (Rich lost the battle) and our little chipmunk visitor who leaves acorns and sunflower seeds in my boots and the clean linen. In spite of all this, everyone tells me I'm doing great for a city girl.

We have grown together as a couple with our new living arrangement and continue to nurture our individual spirits by making a point to spend a day per week apart.

Rich is remodeling his 100-year-old farmhouse and has included me in all the decisions to make it more couple-friendly.

My left-of-center independence is slowly making its way back toward center and I feel more balanced and giving. I am finally in a relationship with a man who loves me the way I have been waiting to be loved my entire life.

We both know that when the time is right and life's circumstances align and obligations subside, we'll find an exotic and romantic place to get married.

That's the beauty of finding love in your 40s, 50s and beyond...you are *so* worth the wait, and so is he.

M.E. JONES is a producer/director/writer. She produced numerous network television series including *The Fresh Prince of Bel Air*, *Moesha*, and *The Wayan Bros.* She is currently writing a book about her experiences as a Hollywood producer. This chapter will be expanded upon in her upcoming book, *Finding Love Way Past 40*. M.E. is currently living in Michigan and still maintains her connection to Southern California. She can be reached at mejonmv@gmail.com.

PART TWO

Strategies

Healing the Heart

Leaning into grief and finding gold

DEBBIE PHILLIPS

It was the first time—the only time—I saw my father cry like that.

I was 10, and the oldest of five kids.

For a March day in the Midwest, it was oddly warm and sunny. Stranger still, my parents told me I didn't have to go to school if I didn't want to. They mentioned this as they rushed out the door, begging us to be good for Connie, our kind and beautiful 16-year-old cousin they had installed to oversee us.

I agonized over the decision, but finally came to the conclusion that I should stay home—just in case something went wrong. What, I had no idea. But I was used to being the big sister, the one in charge, and I had a vague sense that Connie might need re-enforcements.

I spent most of that day shuttling between the sparsely decorated bedroom that I shared with my younger sisters, Lori and Susan, and the cement stoop of our 1960s ranch-style home. One minute nervously biting my nails over the strangeness of the day's events and the next lost in the thoughts of a typical fifth-grader in 1966: Will I be able to get the Beatles' new 45 rpm?

Outside, I soaked in the sunshine and folded my hands in prayer. My heart told me something was amiss; my prayer was that I was wrong.

As the sun slipped away on that incredibly beautiful day, my parents' well-worn Chevrolet sputtered into the driveway.

Connie warned us that we might not want to get too excited and jump all over Mom and Dad when they came through the door.

We ignored her, of course.

As they swept through the back door, we were a tangle of puppies, lapping up every bit of their energy, smothering them in hugs and kisses. I sensed something had changed, but they seemed to appreciate that we hadn't.

Dad asked us to come into their bedroom. Family meetings were usually reserved for special announcements. Were we going to the zoo? A trip to get ice cream? Did they have a present for us?

We sat in a circle on the heirloom bedspread that topped their perfectly made double bed. My normally warm and effusive mother leaned quietly in the doorway.

"I don't know how to tell you this," said Dad. His voice quivered. "Grandma died this morning."

He began to cry. He tried to stop, and it gave way to a sob.

It was shocking. Grandma, my mother's mother, whom I loved so dearly, who always held me close, showered me with sweetness, celebrated my love of strawberry shortcake, had *died*. Even at 10, I knew dying at age 56 was way too young.

And I had never witnessed my father's deepest emotions. Here was the man who only two months earlier, after our new puppy had been poisoned, stoically held me against his chest while I cried with such force and for so long that the entire front of his yellow oxford shirt was soaked. Here he was, holding us and crying.

Until the day he died, nearly 40 years later, surrounded by his tangle of five puppies-turned-middle-age dogs, I never loved him so deeply nor felt so connected to him as I did that night he told us Grandma died, and he cried.

GRIEVING GRANDMA

Grandma's death threw our family for a loop as surely as if a tornado had picked us up, blown us upside down and inside out, and dropped us back onto the landscape. We were still alive, but we were all dazed. Everything was changed. Grandma was missing.

Gone were her delicious, homemade meals. No more family gatherings around the Formica table that dominated her fragrant kitchen.

Sleepovers, strawberry-picking, summer visits—all in the past. Everything seemed dead. Not just Grandma. It hurt so much.

I wanted to scream: "If we all die eventually, doesn't somebody here know how to handle this pain?"

I was terrified my parents would die, too. Every night I prayed and bargained with God. I promised that if my parents would be allowed to live until I was at least 17, when I would be old enough to care for myself and my siblings, I would be very, very good.

I quickly learned that there was a taboo around talking about death. It wasn't a subject to bring up publicly. But why?

In my little-girl mind, I was determined to figure out this "dying thing."

I also was determined that I wasn't going to lose touch with Grandma or let her memory die. Secretly, I marked each month that passed since her death… April 11, May 11, June 11…. With each pencil slash under the lace doily on my dresser, I thought about what I was grateful to Grandma for. I decided I would adopt the part of her I loved best to keep her spirit alive. She was very kind. So I would do my best to follow in her footsteps.

These rituals gave me comfort, but I wanted to know more about how to cope.

I went to our small-town library and asked for books about dying. The librarian did a double-take, as though I'd said something bad.

"People die," she informed me. "But they don't write *books* about it."

I didn't say it, but I thought, "Well, someone should."

I outsmarted her and the Dewey decimal system and somehow located books on reincarnation. All right! There *were* people thinking about what happens after we die.

I searched feverishly for information on this horrible, dizzying, frightening, exhausting, disconnected feeling of losing a loved one.

If I could get through this, I'd figure out a path for others and share it.

Like an explorer, I crept into territory I'd never seen anyone enter before. From sixth grade on, I observed the reactions of others when they lost loved ones. I wrote letters telling them what I valued about the person who died.

I'd look at the newspaper obituaries and multiply every deceased person by 10, figuring there were probably at least that many people affected by each death. It accounted for a lot of people grieving.

I never shied away from asking people about their loved ones' deaths. And most people responded positively to my private and personal outreach. Talking to others about their own grief loosened the grip grief held on me since losing Grandma.

By the time I was a teenager, I saw the gift from Grandma's death. I could talk—or more importantly, listen— to people struggling over death, dying and grief.

It was only one skill in the toolkit I would need for what I was about to take on.

LIFE AS A NEWSPAPER REPORTER

"That was the 'cop shop,'" my city editor chuckled, throwing the brown telephone handset back into its cradle. "They're not too happy that we're ahead of them on their investigation."

We'd surprised and angered police detectives by publishing details of a murder in a front-page story I'd written for that morning's paper.

"I told 'em to get some women detectives who know how to talk to people like our women do." He was filled with pride. I felt on top of the world.

I was in my early 20s and a reporter for a major metropolitan daily newspaper. I could talk to nearly anyone about anything, especially about the toughest subject of all: death.

Over the years, my overwhelming sadness in losing Grandma slowly gave way to a life of promise and excitement. I even had a thrilling prospect in my personal life: a new boyfriend! After dating less than two months, Brad invited me to meet his parents.

MEETING LIBBY

It was the coldest day of the year. Getting ready, I pulled on and off nearly every combination in my closet until I settled on the best I could do—a beige turtleneck sweater under my thin-cotton, cinch-waist dress. I added boots in an attempt to look chic. I wanted his parents' approval.

As I waited to be picked up, I was a wreck. His family lived in the wealthiest part of the city. I was nervous and intimidated. I feared I couldn't measure up.

When Brad arrived, he looked serious. He said he needed to tell me something before I met his parents.

"Remember how I told you my mother was a nurse?" He lowered his voice as though to prepare me for what he must have worried I would find odd. "She takes care of *terminally ill* people."

He might as well have said, "You just won the lottery!"

I was elated. Surely, a nurse who cares for terminally ill people knows about grief. No matter how this relationship worked out, I would actually know someone trained in death and dying. My head spun!

I was relieved. At least I would have one important subject to connect to his mother on—and it was my favorite secret subject.

Arriving at his parents' home, I negotiated the ice that covered the driveway and path to the house. Carefully, I crept up the slippery back porch steps, and the door flew open.

Standing there was a vision of beauty, warmth and welcome. "Hi, I'm Libby Bradford!" she said, smiling at me like a fairy godmother. I loved her instantly.

She reached out and pulled me through the back door, into an entirely new world.

More than two years later, Brad and I were married.

From day one, and for more than a decade, Libby and I talked, laughed, cried, gossiped, strategized and shared stories about our lives and our careers. She listened to me for hours upon hours. We vacationed together. We scheduled frequent lunch and shopping dates. In the peace, beauty and comfort of her living room, we curled up under a mohair blanket.

She bought me my first expensive suit (Austin Reed), taught me to play tennis (my first Prince racket and Tretorn sneakers), took me to my first self-help workshop (Madeline L'Engle) and supported my dreams and goals (to be a successful, independent woman).

Her own life's purpose had become clear when she was a critical-care nurse and witnessed so many people dying in pain and desperation. She believed it was wrong and set out to find a better way. Shortly after turning 50, she discovered a new kind of end-of-life care, and she moved heaven and earth to bring it to her part of the country. Hospice was so unheard of in the United States when Libby led the way that most people mispronounced it "hoe-spice."

It was an exciting time for both of us. As she built an environment and acceptance for hospice, I built my career as a journalist and political press secretary.

During those years, I learned from her about death and dying. She taught me that grief was something to "go through," not to avoid, and that "leaning into grief" could result in amazing personal growth and new and surprising rewards and investments in life.

She shared the profiles of the patients she worked with and how families coped with the support of skilled hospice workers. I was so proud of her.

Everyone loved and admired Libby. She was what I imagined it would be like to have Jackie Kennedy for a mother-in-law. She was elegant, educated, gracious, articulate, and sophisticated, a working woman whose family came first. Plus, she was a great cook with a funny sense of humor and a huge laugh.

I felt loved, supported and cherished by her.

Late in the autumn of my 10th year of life with Libby, she lost weight and was in and out of the emergency room a few times. During one of our frequent lunches, it dawned on me: As a nurse, she might have some idea what was wrong with her.

"Are you OK? Do you know what's wrong?"

I was shocked by her response.

"If I die, you will be OK."

I cried out, "If you die, I will NOT be OK!" And I began to sob.

She quickly and kindly led me out of the restaurant and into her warm car. She settled me down by saying that we'd just have to be patient. She would soon have a liver biopsy and then we'd go from there.

I still have the note I took when my sister-in-law, Lucinda, called as we awaited the results: "Warren says it doesn't look good." Warren was Libby's best friend and colleague. He was not only a physician, but also an oncologist and medical director of hospice. If things were bad, Warren would know.

A few days later, we gathered around Libby and Phil, my father-in-law, in their living room. Warren told us that Libby had a rare condition called amyloidosis. No one diagnosed with amyloidosis had ever lived longer than three years, and Libby's condition was advanced. She would die within a year.

I wanted everything to freeze. I looked into Libby's clear blue eyes. At 60, she looked healthy and as beautiful as ever. The news could not be true. Our Libby *teaches* people about dying; she couldn't *be* dying.

As Libby escorted Warren to the back door, my father-in-law said simply and comfortingly, "God will not give us more than we can bear."

Libby came back into the room and announced, "We are going to have hospice, and it will be a beautiful death."

LIBBY'S DYING

"Your kids were here today," Libby said sweetly and matter-of-factly.

"Oh, really? How many do I have?"

Libby had prepared me for her dying process. With a nurse's clarity, she described how her physical symptoms would unfold. The aspect she dreaded most would be when her body would eventually fill with toxins and she would be "daffy in the head."

"Three," she answered. "They were so good. They were playing over there." She pointed to an empty corner of the room.

I smiled. Even if Brad and I were to have children, I could never imagine three.

"They're blonde," she added.

I didn't have the heart to tell her that blonde children also were highly unlikely. I come from dark-haired people.

Warren's prediction of Libby's life expectancy came true. Libby lived for eight months, and during that time we laughed and cried, cleaned out closets, wrote good-bye notes and gave gifts to people she loved. We even drew up a list of women acceptable for Phil to marry! She faced her death squarely, and she led me through it with her.

Cared for by the hospice doctors and nurses she had trained, Libby died peacefully at home in her own bed. I lay beside her, holding her left hand. Surrounding her bed, our family chanted her request of "Forget-me-nots-in-Heaven" as she took her last breaths, just feet from where she had "seen" my children playing.

GRIEVING LIBBY

In the weeks following Libby's death, I felt a sense of accomplishment. There had been much "anticipatory grief," another fine concept I learned from her. The gift of limited time allows people the opportunity for closure, and in her dying, Libby guided us in working through all the steps:

I forgive you.

Please forgive me.

I love you.

Thank you.

Goodbye.

One night shortly before Libby died, she pulled me closer to her on the bed.
"Everything's going to be OK."
I wasn't sure if she was asking a question or giving an answer.
"You'll be fine."
Libby knew my long-held dream to attend graduate school in Boston when I was done working in politics. I had been planning and preparing so I could take off the year-plus required, if I were accepted.
When Libby died, she left the money for my tuition and expenses. I could go to school a year earlier than I'd anticipated. In the midst of the sadness, I felt a window of joy and huge gratitude to her.
I applied and was accepted at Harvard's Kennedy School.
But once I arrived in Boston, my heartache set in deeply. I couldn't escape the despair of missing Libby. I needed help. But where could I

get it? And who could give it? I was too private and fearful to share my excruciating pain.

Late one afternoon, I felt I would suffocate. I searched the Yellow Pages for "grief counselor." I used every conceivable, similar topic and found nothing to help someone in the throes of grief. Raging, I ripped out pages and flung the massive book across the room. I screamed and cried and sobbed to exhaustion.

To comfort myself, I drew a bath ... and very seriously thought that it would not take much to slip under the water and out of the agony.

I thought about the children in my life. While I did not have children of my own, there were children who were very important to me. I could not do that to them.

LEANING INTO THE GRIEF

The help I needed came in many forms. I learned to meditate. I went to therapy. The book *The Courage to Grieve* by Judy Tatelbaum gave me comfort. I found solace in nature on Martha's Vineyard, the island Libby introduced me to.

I attended inspiring workshops and seminars such as Dr. Brian Weiss's past-life regression and James Van Praagh's "Talking To Heaven." I traveled to Bali with spiritual teacher Marianne Williamson. I discovered formulas that helped me through, such as this one from Dr. Mark Goulston:

RECIPE TO GRIEVE

Cry
Scream
Shriek
Sob
Reach into yourself
Reach out to others
Take a deep breath
Whimper
Rest
Repeat often, and until you know you will be OK.

While I was healing, people in my life gave me unexpected joy. My dear friends Christopher and Melanie gave birth to Eleanor just a few months after Libby died. And later they had Max. I loved every second playing with and caring for the children. I took every opportunity to be with them.

Phil did not marry any of the women on Libby's list, but he married a woman Libby liked very much. In the same house that Phil lived in for more than 50 years, 40 of them shared with Libby, he and Renate filled their days with fun, travel, music, love, laughter, cats, cake and coffee.

When Eleanor and Max had a sister, Julia, Christopher and Melanie asked me to be her godmother.

Going over to Phil and Renate's was always a big treat for the children because there was so much fun and activity.

Plus, they were allowed to jump up and down on the high, four-poster bed with the fluffy down quilts! The room and bed Libby died in was once again a happy place. On one visit, to great laughter and abandon, I was throwing the children onto the big bed and they were bouncing off of it. Out of the corner of my eye, I saw all three fall onto the floor on top of each other.

Three little blonde angels laughing and shrieking, filling the empty space Libby had pointed to so long ago. Tears splashed down my face.

"Debbie, why are you crying?" asked Eleanor, 6. "This is so fun."

And, that's the day "my" three, blonde children learned about happy tears.

DEBBIE PHILLIPS is the founder of the Women on Fire™ organization. A pioneer in the field of life and executive coaching, she became a coach in 1995. She has been a radio and newspaper reporter, governor's press secretary and executive of a television production company. In 1998, she created Vision Day®, the personal strategic planning day for your life. She is married to Rob Berkley and, with Wilber the cat, they live in Martha's Vineyard, Mass., and Naples, Fla.

Learning Knows No Age Limit

How passion and perseverance finally led me to a college degree

JACQUELINE ANN PIMENTEL

When I was asked to participate in the *Women on Fire* project, I was immediately humbled, thinking, "Why would anyone want to read my story? What could anyone possibly gain from it?" But then I remembered what my dear friend and mentor Dr. Robert Nevin used to remind me: "When they are passing tarts, Jacqueline, take a tart!" Over the years, I have learned to trust that, when an opportunity is presented, it is no mistake. Moreover, the gifts gained and how they manifest themselves are beyond imagining. They are simply waiting for me to take a leap of faith. So here I go....

Even though I've had a long, successful career as a real-estate broker on Martha's Vineyard, there was something missing in my life, some unfinished business from my errant youth that I needed to take care of. You see, I had dropped out of college 30 years earlier and, during all my years of success, I felt that I never truly measured up because I didn't have a degree. So when I turned 50, the time seemed right to make my dream a reality.

THE FIRST STEP

On Jan. 1, 2001, I moved into a pied-à-terre in Boston, initially to get away from the winter doldrums on Martha's Vineyard and even perhaps to look for something new and different to do with my life. My deep interest in art had been recently reawakened, and I was traveling back and forth from Martha's Vineyard to Boston to take painting and drawing courses at the Museum of Fine Arts. The occasional lectures I attended about the museum's collection or other art-related topics inspired and thrilled me.

One day as I was walking around the city in a joyful haze, I passed an office with a sign in the window saying the company worked with adults interested in returning to college. I went in. After a short meeting with a counselor, I left with some reading material and a tingle of excitement. I wondered if it could be possible, if I could really return to college after such a long absence.

When it came to what I wanted to study, I knew without question it would be art history. I learned that Harvard University—Harvard University!—offered an undergraduate degree program for people just like me. Of course I thought it was ridiculous to even consider myself going to Harvard, but I went to check out the program anyway.

Next thing I knew, I was meeting with a university adviser and enrolling in my first course. Acceptance into the program was predicated on achieving a B or better in a minimum of three courses in my chosen field of study. To begin, I enrolled in only one course to see if I could actually handle the work and the life of a college student while working full time. The course, "Caravaggio and Bernini," looked at two of Italy's masters in painting and sculpture. At the time, I didn't know who these men were, but I soon found myself falling in love with them, as well as with every other aspect of college life.

My first day as a student on campus will stay with me forever. I arrived early, complete with a new backpack, pens, notebooks and a map of where to go. I was terrified that I would end up in the wrong class. As I stood in the middle of Harvard Yard, gazing up in awe at the sweep of steps leading to the majestic Widener Library, I felt like genuflecting. When I located my building and lecture hall, I went straight to a seat in the front and center of the room (a position I claimed in all of my classes for the duration), as I didn't want to miss a single pearl of wisdom that would be proffered before me. The professor arrived, handed out a syllabus and the lecture began. I sat in mesmerized rapture. I was hooked.

We had several papers to write for that class and, because I hadn't written an academic paper in a very long time, I didn't even know where to begin. The first assignment was to write a paper covering a series of questions using the lecture notes and material we were reading. I neatly numbered and retyped the questions, then wrote an answer addressing each point the professor asked us to consider. OK, so it was a good version of a fifth-grade project and not what the professor expected of a college student. Thank goodness, it was not graded, and the professor was gentle with his remarks. He wrote that, although I made a good effort to answer the questions, in the future he expected the assignments completed in essay form. I was red with shame, but brave enough to go up and tell him that this was my first college class after a very long "sabbatical," and that I hadn't quite understood the assignment. He suggested that I avail myself of the writing tutor program offered by the college. I immediately signed up.

Turning back was no longer an option. I was on my way to my coveted degree.

Living as an undergraduate coed in my 50s was an invigorating experience. I think it might even be better than having cosmetic surgery, as every semester people kept telling me how much younger I looked. Not that life back in college wasn't sometimes painful; it was. But I didn't have to go under the knife or get poisonous injections to regain some of my youthful exuberance. Outfitted in jeans, boots, backpack, and sometimes a mink coat, crossing the Harvard campus to class, I had a sense of belonging and purpose. I would smile and think to myself, "I can't believe I'm doing this!"

TRIAL BY FIRE

The next hurdle I faced that first semester was the midterm exam. I didn't know how to study for a test of this caliber. I was a wreck, and I remember wondering where to begin. I couldn't imagine how I was ever going to remember all the material. "What if I fail? I can't possibly do this!" was some of the negative chatter renting space in my head. Thankfully, I had a 20-year-old niece who was completing her senior year at Suffolk University, and she happened to be taking an art history course covering some of the same material. She came to my apartment and set me up with note cards and a study format. Then we began to question and test each other's knowledge. This was the first of many interesting, stimulating and critical study groups I participated in throughout my undergraduate career.

The day of my first final exam at Harvard, I was excited and nervous. As I headed to school on the subway, a friend called to wish me luck. "Break a leg!" she told me. I got a chill down my spine when she said it.

I was hours early for the exam, so I went directly to the fine arts library to cram any last bits of knowledge I could possibly fit into my saturated brain. I looked around at all the hunched over bodies surrounded by books and notes, absorbed in the last-second study ritual. It seemed surreal that I was there with those obviously brilliant students, about to get my baptism by fire. I found a spot, opened my books and notes, and settled in to study.

At one point, I went to stand, but as I got up from my seat, my foot curled under my ankle. I hit the floor…right there in the fine arts library at Harvard. I was humiliated. In that quiet sanctuary, the noise caused enough of a stir that most of the students jumped up and rushed over to see how I was. Wishing to dissolve and disappear into the carpet, I said I was fine. But my ankle was beginning to swell up like a balloon. I struggled to my feet and hobbled my way outside. Next door at the faculty club, I found ice to lay on my poor injured ankle.

Although I was in pain and totally distracted, I resolved not to miss or postpone my exam. I limped back to the library and put my ice-swaddled leg up on a chair. I tried to calm down and concentrate. As the time for the exam loomed, I hopped across the street to Emerson Hall, full of dread and foreboding, thinking myself a complete idiot. There were a few minutes before we were allowed to enter the room, so I laid down on my back on a hallway floor and put my leg up on the wall to help relieve the pressure. As I lay there, my leg pulsating with pain, my professor rounded the corner, looked down at me quizzically and asked, "What happened to you?" Great start.

Miraculously, I did well on the exam. I knew I was in this now for the long haul. I ended that semester in good standing, hungry to learn more and keep going.

Because I am my sole provider, I needed to work full time while going to school. My profession as a real-estate broker afforded me the flexibility and income stream to continue my studies. But with my primary home and job being on Martha's Vineyard, I had to allow for plenty of travel time. Many people asked how I could do this, or even why I wanted to do this. But it didn't feel like a sacrifice to me at all. I was inspired, excited and totally committed to making it happen. I just made the best use of my time as I traveled back and forth to Cambridge by boat, car and/or bus. I would get permission to tape the lectures and listen to them during my commute to reinforce what I had learned in class.

Another way I discovered to help impress all of the information onto my brain was by being part of a study group. I found it surprisingly enjoyable. Each session entailed not only the intense focus and effort to recall and make sense of the material we had covered over a period of six to eight weeks, but we also needed to find suitable niches that would accommodate our bodies, books, notes, drinks and other study paraphernalia.

Ever the adventuress, I generally took it upon myself to scout out the coveted study locales. Once I even prevailed upon the dean to let us use his personal conference room, because it was the only private, noise-free space on campus to be had. My classmates shook their heads in disbelief, but they were extremely grateful for our quiet zone for the cram session. Other members of my study groups were also impressed with my grasp of the material. It used to blow me away that the other students would look to me as some kind of "smarty-pants egghead." I'd never viewed myself in that way, ever.

STUDY ABROAD

As I walked between classes, amid the ads and articles plastered to the bulletin boards all over campus, I would see notices for opportunities to study abroad. I kept thinking, "Oh man, would I love to do this! It would certainly flesh out my undergrad experience." So, once I had my academic performance jitters under control, I launched full steam into researching the different programs offered all around the world for undergraduates. I finally chose a program offered in Portugal because it is the home of my father's ancestors.

As soon as I had made this decision, I tracked down the professors who would be teaching the course. I launched an email campaign to introduce myself and to set up appointments to learn the requirements for the 2004 summer semester. They needed a review of my grades and an essay. I got my interview, wrote my essay and was accepted!

Off I went to the seaside resort town of Cascais, Portugal. My roommate was a 19-year-old woman from Poland who was about to begin her senior year at Harvard. We both laughed when I told her that she was my first college roommate.

We were a group of only 14 students and two professors, one a chair of the literature department at Harvard. I was older than one of the professors and certainly senior to all of my fellow classmates, but I never felt like an adult. Day after day, the experiences grew richer in scholarship, friendship, fun and cultural enlightenment.

What a blast that semester was! Of course I took a different approach than that of my fellow classmates in how to share in this unique experience. For the most part, I chose to skip the all-night reveling in order to study and be clear-headed for classes the next day. I'm certainly not a prude, and there was a time when I would have been right in the middle of the pack, but three decades wiser, I wanted to be fully present for the incredible learning opportunity that stood before me.

Toward the end of our semester in Portugal, we were assigned essays to replace a final exam. There were three papers, totaling 30 pages, due on topics of our choice from the material covered. The entire grade rested on the quality of these academic papers. Most evenings after classes, I'd take to my room and work on the assignments. Many times I'd see the doorknob turn, and one of my young classmates would come into my room for a chat. I learned to say, "If you don't have anything to add to my paper, get out of my room!" At which point they'd reply, "Stop working so hard! You are going to ruin the grading curve!" But I was able to finish up the semester's work with plenty of time left to explore the beautiful countryside, free from academic pressure, while my 20-something colleagues were pulling all-nighters. I cherish and relish every delicious memory of that long-desired, college experience abroad.

Back on the Harvard campus that fall, I was a junior. What most impressed me was the lofty thinking and deep intellectual discussions on every imaginable topic that took place daily. I swear that if you stand still in the middle of Harvard Yard, you can feel the energy of all the thinking coursing through the air! This atmosphere inspired me to seek out and participate in a variety of lectures and seminars inside and outside of my field of concentration. I once sat in on a weekend seminar on entrepreneurship given by professors and graduate students of Harvard's world-class business school. I took full advantage of the phenomenal array of scholastic, cultural and artistic opportunities to round out my college experience. Sporting events, too. Tailgating at the Harvard/Yale football game was and continues to be a fun affair.

Having gained confidence in my academic capabilities, I even boldly challenged one of the teaching assistants who gave me a B on a paper that I felt deserved an A. I set up an appointment to defend my thesis, arguments, reasoning and evidence. He offered me a compromise and asked me to rewrite portions of the paper to bring up my grade. My self-confidence took a huge leap from this encounter.

There was not any one particular "Aha" moment that I can remember during my life at Harvard. It was more a continuing series of small awakenings every time I sat in a lecture hall taking notes or conducted research in any of the extraordinary libraries and art museums. I would get lost for hours on end in these wonderful places. With my student ID and directives from my professors, I was given entree and special attention at other Boston museums. Time stood still for me as I became so absorbed in my studies and in the flow of the now.

MISSION ACCOMPLISHED

And, then it happened.

After four and a half years, 18 classes and numerous new college friends, I graduated. I stood fifth in my class for academic achievement and was inducted into a national honor society. Furthermore, I was appointed to be one of the two class marshals to lead my class for Harvard's 350th graduation ceremony. That day, as my name was called and I walked across the stage to receive my diploma and congratulations from the dean, is one of my proudest moments in a life filled with many blessings.

Today, I feel complete having achieved this milestone. I have even considered going for my master's degree.

At present I am formulating a business plan to launch a small educational service to help people look at and learn about art. It's still in the infancy stages of planning and development, and I am getting great feedback on the idea from professionals in the field.

For any of you who have ever thought about returning to college to complete a degree program as I did or even starting at the very beginning, listen to your heart. You know what my old friend Doc Nevin would say: When they are passing tarts…take a tart!

JACQUELINE ANN PIMENTEL continues to pursue her fine arts education, in addition to her real estate brokerage work on Martha's Vineyard. A member of the fine arts committee at the Harvard Club of Boston, she helps to plan and organize fine arts events. She travels the world in search of great art. She can be reached at jpiment10@gmail.com to help lead you back to school, talk about art or lure you to the Vineyard.

Breaking Loose from Corporate America

Seven secrets to surviving being let go from your job

SHANNON M. McCAFFERY

My life was somewhat scarred and forever changed the first time I was let go from Corporate America. I was one of those people who thought I would work at the same place for 25 years and then happily retire. On the contrary, the more determined I was to stay in one place, the more the Universe upended my quest for a steady stream of employment. In fact, I was laid off not once, not twice, not three times, but four times before something remarkable happened in my career.

Let me pull back the curtain to reveal the somewhat tragic time in my life that I now fondly refer to as "my career transition rollercoaster ride." It all began when the company I worked for was being sold, and my dream job as director of international marketing came to an end. The job was a dream not only because I got to see the world, traveling to such places as Bali, Kuala Lumpur, Singapore, Australia, Amsterdam, Cannes and Bangkok, but also because I ran a department of four people, a position that included motivating, training, hiring and firing (talk about challenging). And I managed a fiscal budget of more than $500,000. We were a new department, and I relished taking all of the innovative efforts we were doing in the United States and sharing them with our international counterparts.

One of the other great parts of that job was that I met and got to know one of the top executives in the company, Rob Berkley, who later would become a champion and mentor for me and an inspiring force in my life. Rob was also instrumental in introducing me to Debbie Phillips, who became my executive coach. And, boy, did I need one. She helped me tremendously throughout all my career transitions.

HOME LIFE CRUMBLES

As my career was changing, virtually disintegrating before my eyes, so paralleled my marriage. My husband and I had been together for eight years and, although we had no kids, we owned our own home and were parents to two golden retrievers. I found it ironic that, as I started to really take stock of my career and make changes in my life, everything else started to crumble around me. I felt I was watching an avalanche in slow motion. Thankfully, I'd built up a strong support system of friends who saw me through to the bitter end. This was where I discovered **my first secret to surviving life's major transitions: "You have to have support!"** This was a lifesaver for me: having a coach, therapist, family, friends and my dogs. It was incredibly helpful to know I was not alone. I worked hard at not being afraid to ask for help and at telling my support system what I needed and how they could help me.

After I survived my first career transition of the company being sold, I wound up back in a marketing position in the same company, in the U.S. division. I happily stayed there for more than a year and enjoyed traveling and working with our teams around the United States. Then a fabulous new position in another division of the company landed in my lap, and I jumped at the chance to take it. The new position focused on Internet marketing and using technology to sell products. I traveled to various countries, discovering many new things about training on the Web. I loved my position.

But after being there for three months, the rug was pulled out from under my feet. The vice president came to me and said she wasn't sure I was right for this position. What a jaw-dropper for me! I could feel the tears welling up in my eyes. My mouth shot open so wide that, if there had been a fly in the room, I'm sure it would have landed inside. I couldn't fathom that this position wasn't the right fit for me. I'd given it more than 100 percent. The only words that came out of my mouth were, "Well, what should we do about this?" In my numbed stupor, I could see her mouth moving, but I couldn't hear or comprehend what she was saying. I was sure she was speaking another language. She had her mind made up and encouraged me to take another position within the company. The irony is that she said I was an asset and she didn't want to lose me altogether.

After I left her office in utter shock and disbelief, I picked up the phone and frantically dialed Debbie. I desperately needed my support system. As miracles do happen, she answered the phone, and all of my feelings of failure, helplessness and disbelief came spilling out in mountains of words and sobs. This moment in my life was huge, larger than anything I could have ever expected. The shock shook me to my core. The timing was terrible because I also was going through a divorce. Ugh. I so believed that my job defined "me"—it was my life. Without a job, I had no identity.

This was where I discovered **my second secret to surviving life's major transitions: "Tame the mind."** When I was facing these big changes, I found that my mind was my worst enemy. I needed to work on taming it, so I took up the practice of meditation. I read books about it, and then I went to Kripalu Center for Yoga and Health in Lenox, Mass., where I learned more about how to quiet and calm my mind. It was really difficult at first, but with inspiration and support, it became more natural to me. It also worked wonders in helping me to relax. I was able to better control my thoughts and not let my mind run amok with bad thoughts that weren't even remotely helpful to me in my state of job loss.

I'd been going at breakneck, bullet-train speed for years, working with no real breaks. The fear of not being employed and going into an office every day was scary to me. What would I do with myself? Yikes! My choices at this point were to get another job within the company or take a three-month severance package and leave. Even though I would later find out that the whole department was shut down and everyone was let go, my emotions were still screaming at me that I somehow had failed.

GIFT OF TIME

With courage and strength from my support system, I convinced myself that it was OK to risk not having a job to go to for a time. I took the three-month severance package. What a concept! Not working for three months and getting paid for it! I was elated and freaked out at the same time, and I didn't know what to do with myself. A good friend suggested I view this as a gift of time to figure out where I needed to be. I had nothing to lose. I just needed to follow and trust my intuition.

This job loss might not have been so painful if that was all I was dealing with at the time. Right after I was laid off, I learned that the house I had been renting since my separation was going to be sold. In just a matter of weeks, I found myself with no husband, no job and no place to live. And how would I find a place to live when I had no job? To make matters even more complicated, one of the key players of my support system—my best friend—and I had a falling out. I felt isolated, alone and basically hopeless.

So what did I do when I was down and out and feeling hopeless? I booked myself for some incredible, life-changing travel. Here's my **third secret to surviving life's major transitions: "Take yourself on vacation!"** I decided to get on a plane, by myself, knowing no one, and go to Peru. This was the best thing I could ever have done for my psyche: change scenery and shake things up a bit. I got all my shots up-to-date, obtained pills for elevation sickness (I would be 9,000-12,000 feet above sea level) and fit all my necessities into a small duffle bag. I also purchased some great hiking gear and lots of bug spray. After two weeks of getting everything in order, I was off on a plane to Houston, then to Lima, and then a small plane to Cuzco, Peru. For 12 days, I hiked and meditated in the Andes. Experiencing Machu Picchu with a group of spiritually inclined people (I had been recommended a tour group called Magical Journey by some dear friends) was incredibly inspiring to me. This was the journey my workaholic soul needed to help me open up to my life.

Sometimes I was so far out of my comfort zone that my skin crawled. Yet, I wasn't going to let my fear paralyze me from my new life's exploration. And that brings me to my **fourth secret to surviving life's transitions: "Feel your fear; it's OK."** This was huge for me because I was so scared about not knowing how I was going to pull through with all these transitions hitting me at once. I cried an awful lot, and meditated so much I had visions. I found the land in Peru to be unbelievably spiritual, and I became very connected to it. I could feel the energy in everything I touched. I came to realize that not only did I want to live my life differently, but I wanted to be able to tell my tale and possibly even help others in the process.

After living for 12 days in jeans, shorts and hiking boots, eating real food grown from the land with no preservatives, and connecting with people and my higher power on a spiritual level, I was thrust back into the reality of living in the New York metropolitan area. To cope with the contrast of my newfound spirituality, I started using my deeply focused skills of meditation, affirmations and visualizations to help get me through the shell shock of my harsh reality. My mantra became, "I'll find the perfect job and perfect home for me and my dogs by Nov. 1." This is the date I had to find a job and move by. I repeated this sentence out loud and in my mind about 40-50 times a day while walking my dogs, meditating, and going about my day. My **fifth secret to surviving life's major transitions came into play heavily here: "Reach out to experts!"** I can't say enough about having a coach, a therapist and any other specialist that can help you see your way through a transition. Yet, it's not just about having them in your life, but about picking up the phone and "asking" them for help.

I hope you're sitting down because this might floor you: My meditations and visualizations worked! I found a job and a home by the exact date that I had declared in my mantra. My support system came through in every way. I found a place to live, plus my old company that had just let me go hired me back! The job was a newly created position of director of corporate communications. During my tenure, I discovered a whole new side of my potential and expanded my capabilities in many ways.

After three years of helping the company outsource and lay off people, it was my turn (yes, again!) to be laid off with 20 other people. This time, to be fair, I had a really good heads-up that this was going to happen. But it still didn't make the process any easier or less emotionally charged to go through. Once again I was out of Corporate America, and I had no clue what to do next. I tried starting my own business, but I was just not focused and couldn't handle the instability of not getting a regular paycheck. Plus, I really missed being in an office.

It took me 10 months to find something, and it was only a temporary consulting position. During this transition, I discovered **surviving life's major transitions secret number six: "Indulge in self-soothing."** When my world was in transition once again, I learned the best thing for me to do was figure out how to soothe myself. It came in many different dimensions, from aromatherapy (candles, incense and soaps) to baths, body lotions, flowers and ice cream. There are tons of things you can do, when you focus, to make yourself smile, laugh and feel good inside.

The consulting job was interesting—a totally different animal. The company hired me to be their corporate communications consultant for six weeks. And after that time was up, they hired me on permanently. They knew a fantastic workaholic when they saw one! They convinced me to be their event marketer and learn the ins and outs of event marketing and planning. This definitely stretched my skills even further, yet the downsides were big. The job was exhausting, the hours were insane, and the constant travel was getting to me. I became convinced this job was taking years off my life.

MAKING TIME FOR MYSELF

In fact, I did end up having to go the hospital for some minor surgery (turns out this job was making me ill) and had to take off some time to recuperate. Then it happened. I got my sign from the Universe. I was scheduled to go back to work after two weeks of recuperating when I got a call from the office. I could almost feel it in the air. Once again, I was being let go. The division was having problems and they were reducing staff. This was where my **secret number seven to surviving life's major transitions came into play: "It is all about comforting the body."** I scheduled regular massages and cranio-sacral bodywork to get my mind and body tuned for my latest transition. Your body keeps a lot of things in during major transitions and change, so you need to do what you can to take good care of it. You need to get lots of rest, exercise and take in a massage…or two or three.

So the neon sign from the Universe flashed before me for the fourth and final time. I got the message! Being an event marketer certainly wasn't my life's work. Indeed, the fourth time I was let go was the charm. If they hadn't let me go, I might never have left, and I would have been stuck in a miserable job forever. In Corporate America, I went above and beyond on every occasion and poured my heart and soul into this position and countless others. I had my new gift of time and adventure and made a decision: I was not going back to that lifestyle. It had left me four times, and I was done abiding by its rules and the chains that bound me.

I needed to get out of the traditional nine-to-five work and make my mark. I had always loved marketing, coaching and working with inspiring people. I really wanted to make a difference by working with entrepreneurs, information marketers and business owners. Plus, I truly enjoyed helping them make their businesses incredibly successful. I decided to start my own direct-response marketing, coaching and consulting business. Again, a mentor helped me find my way. I received some wonderful inspiration and guidance from my friend and master coach Rob Berkley, who introduced me to millionaire-maker and direct-response marketing guru Dan Kennedy. Discovering Dan's wonderful truths and money-making ideas really opened my eyes to enormous entrepreneurial opportunities.

Starting my own business using direct-response marketing techniques, combined with my experience in coaching, marketing, sales and management in Corporate America allowed me to combine my talents and skills. I not only work with entrepreneurs, information marketers, and business owners to increase the impact of their advertising, I also take their great ideas that they don't have time to work on and implement those ideas for them. I'm truly enjoying my business, working and coaching some incredible people and having the time of my life.

Who would have thought I could break out of the old way of thinking that had me chained to a desk and working for someone else with only two weeks off a year? I learned that wasn't the only way to make money. In addition to my marketing business, I'm also in the process of building two other businesses: one for my passionate hobby, photography, and the other a coaching program for women in transition. I'm now truly on fire with investing in myself, my business and my family. I'm in a rewarding relationship now, and we have son. I am living my life on my terms. I have slammed the door shut on Corporate America and there is no turning back. Independence, perseverance, enthusiasm, passion and success are my bosses now.

SHANNON M. MCCAFFERY, chief marketing implementer for McCaffery Communications, has more than 20 years' experience in coaching, marketing, communications, marketing implementation, management and sales. She has worked for several Fortune 500 companies, including Cendant, Simon & Schuster International and Pearson. She can accurately assess your marketing needs, pinpointing areas and ideas to increase its impact and generate higher profits. Visit Shannon's website at www.MarketingImplementer.com.

'Til Death Do Us Part

How one couple's vow endured divorce and worse

KACY COOK

Sometimes love survives despite all efforts to the contrary.

I met Doug in 1981 when we both worked at a newspaper in Ohio. If not love at first sight, it was certainly a fast-moving relationship. We were living together within a couple of months and married nine months after our introduction.

Doug was flat-out handsome, a cross between Mikhail Baryshnikov and F. Scott Fitzgerald. He had a wicked wit and a knack for mimicry, which he used to devastating effect. He once had a fellow reporter convinced that she was talking to Jimmy Carter on the phone (I'm looking at you, Debbie Phillips). But he also had a curious mind and a serious intellect. His journalism background led him to electronic media in the early days of the field, and he was a pioneer in online publications and interactive media.

FAMILY LIFE

When we bought our first house, Doug took up new interests. He loved to garden and landscape, turning our yard into something of a neighborhood attraction. And could the man ever cook! But back then, for whatever reason, he didn't want anyone to know it. I happily took credit for his work. My favorite "scam" was when his parents would visit. I'd spend the morning primping (well, I did clean the house), while he put together a fabulous meal with impeccable presentation. At the last minute, I'd put on an apron and start memorizing ingredients. Doug would still be in the shower when his parents arrived, and they'd think I pulled off some minor miracle in the kitchen while their son slept in.

After our daughter, Leah, was born in 1983, Doug helped me establish myself as a freelance copy editor. Working from home was just my style—even when it meant getting up at 2 a.m. to finish a project before my parenting skills were required. I had the routine down by the time Jacob was born in 1986 and Ben in 1988.

One evening, Doug handed me a copy of *Utne Reader*. "What do you think of this?" The article was on homeschooling, and I knew immediately I wanted to do it. This was the early '90s and homeschooling was uncommon. But we loved the freedom and togetherness it gave us. We traveled, volunteered and threw ourselves into things we loved— music, art, baseball and nature topped our list. The children excelled in the annual achievement tests they took with their schooled peers. Homeschooling suited us.

THE DARK SIDE

Life wasn't all sunny. Doug waged an ongoing battle with depression, marked by severe insomnia and a deep insecurity. Midnight panic attacks terrified and confused me. Our lives were happy, weren't they?

When in depression's throes, Doug would call from work, desperate for comfort I seemed unable to give. Evenings, he'd lie on the floor and pound his forehead with his fist. He became obsessed with even the smallest details of his health. One summer it was floaters, those tiny specks that drift almost imperceptibly across the line of vision. Doug would hold one eye shut and jerk his head, watching what he called a "shower" of the spots. Then he'd repeat with the other eye. He did this over and over, dozens of times an hour, convinced of impending blindness.

The depressions would eventually lift and, at first, he might go a couple years between recurrences. Then they began coming faster. And something else crept into the cycle: hostility. Once Doug started to recover, he could be abusive in his need to control—in-your-face screaming, threats, breaking things.

There were good years and difficult ones, but family always came first. Until around our 15th year of marriage, when Doug began spending long hours away from home. He said he felt a depression coming on. "Gary's helping me to get a grip," he said of a new friend. I was devastated by Doug's turning to someone else for solace.

As his disappearances dragged on, I suspected Doug was having an affair. I'd sometimes awaken to hear whispered phone calls in the night. But the next morning, I'd press REDIAL and be connected to Gary's number. Maybe Doug was telling the truth after all.

One day I was confessing the painful state of my marriage to my sister. Unexpectedly, from deep within, I suddenly understood: Doug was gay.

It took me weeks to confront him. He denied it at first, his voice too calm, too courteous for the circumstances. Then slowly he started to unload.

Oddly, perhaps, it came as a relief. For one thing, I had felt confused for so long. Every time I'd think I uncovered some truth about what was going on, Doug would convince me I was wrong. I felt I couldn't trust my own mind, that *it* was deceiving me, not Doug. "I can't see what I'm looking at," I told my sister. But I *had* been right. I wasn't crazy.

And somehow it was easier that it wasn't another woman. I suppose my vanity suffered a bit less.

Doug wanted to stay married. He truly loved me, he said. Besides, the way we lived depended on a traditional family pattern. We tried to make it work. But gradually we realized the arrangement wasn't enough for either of us.

EVERYTHING CHANGES, THEN AGAIN AND AGAIN

As we moved toward separation, our professional lives also changed. My freelance editing work grew into a full-time job as senior editor of a science journal. Doug joined a "new media" company with a colleague, which began as a sideline before becoming his central focus.

When the inevitable could be put off no longer, Doug moved out. At first he rented a small apartment, but then he moved in with Gary.

My job had flextime hours, and Doug could work some hours from home, so we tried to balance the homeschooling at first. But it was definitely not the same. So at 16, Leah began taking courses at the community college. We enrolled Jacob and Ben, then 14 and 12, to start school in the fall. Until then, we enlisted extra help. It even turned out Gary was a great math tutor.

Things were changing, had changed, and we were OK. But even as our adjustments were becoming easier, the cold grip of depression again tightened. I instinctively cringed as I waited for the other shoe to drop.

I didn't have long to wait. After a civil, even friendly separation of two years, Doug suddenly filed for divorce. Shockingly, he obtained an emergency custody order by claiming that I was neglecting the children's education.

The order was quickly reversed, but the stage was set for a nasty, prolonged court battle that was costly on so many levels. Hardly a word was exchanged between us that wasn't filtered through attorneys. The divorce dragged on, but we agreed on nothing. The final decree was decided for us: Everything—our assets and debts, the custody of our children—was simply split. Our house was to be sold and the equity divided. We allowed everything we had built together to collapse under the weight of our rancor.

But another blow was about to save us from ourselves.

As I looked for a realtor, my mother was diagnosed with breast cancer. There was surgery and weeks of radiation and chemotherapy ahead of us. I couldn't face that test while packing up 20 years of memories and selling my home.

I asked Doug if I could buy out his equity share and stay in the house. "Of course," he said. Things weren't instantly all better between us, but his understanding and willing assistance helped me through a difficult time.

A while later, I was surprised to learn that Doug was looking at houses to rent. He and Gary weren't breaking up, he told me, just cooling down. But it soon became clear that they had split. Doug found an adorable little house near mine and threw himself into fixing it up.

STEEP DECLINE

The depression that followed Doug's breakup with Gary was his worst ever. He couldn't work, couldn't even see family or friends. He'd lie on the couch all day with the blinds shut against the sun, watching the Food Network and burning through his share of the home equity money. Even for the depths of a depression, this was unusual, to say the least. He was always responsible and dedicated. It was inconceivable that he would just give up. Moreover, he started to drink heavily. He had never been a teetotaler, but this, too, was alarmingly out of character.

One day I allowed myself a moment of self-pity and—I'll admit it—bitterness in front of the kids. I bemoaned the fact that Doug dealt so much better with our breakup than he did his and Gary's. "Look at him!" I said. "He's absolutely losing it over Gary."

"If it makes you feel any better, Mom," Jacob said, "when *I* go insane it'll be because of you."

"Thanks, dear."

Dark, gallows humor was a family staple, our favorite coping method. But we were deeply concerned.

Although I tried to get Doug to help himself, I knew what we were up against. Over the years, he had tried every type of antidepressant and therapy. Nothing helped. Maybe even more frustrating to him was the condescension and skepticism he received when he told people that he was trying.

Doug became so despondent that I asked him to move back into my home, under the condition that he not drink. I actually saw an upside for me. I imagined coming home to dinner in the oven. And since Doug had moved out, my lawn looked like the front yard on *Malcolm in the Middle*—neglected, almost desolate. It would be good for Doug, too, I thought, if he immersed himself in these once favorite pastimes.

But expectations didn't fit reality. Doug just moved to my couch, expecting me to care for him. After a couple months, the kids told me that as soon as I was out the door for work, before they left for school, they could hear the pop of beer cans opening. I couldn't allow this. I insisted that Doug move back to the rented house, which he was still paying for.

During the divorce, Gary had become my sworn enemy. Still, I was consoled when he called one day to express his alarm over the depth of Doug's illness. After that, we spoke fairly regularly.

NOWHERE TO TURN

Doug went downhill shockingly fast. Within months, Doug, who had always been handsome and well dressed, looked like the worst stereotype of the homeless man—bone thin, filthy, with straggly hair and beard. Most days he'd walk aimlessly, sometimes until his feet were bloody, carrying a liter of cheap vodka tucked in a paper bag.

Even with Doug out of our home, I couldn't shield the children from the truth.

When Jacob turned 18, he needed his father's signature to get control of a bank account. I arranged a visit. There was no answer when we knocked, but we heard sounds from inside. Jacob remembered where Doug hid an extra key, and we let ourselves in. We called to Doug. There was no response, but we heard noises overhead. We found Doug cowering in a dark, dirty storage space under the eaves. Doug tried to pull himself up but needed help. Jacob's shock at the sight of his father was obvious and profound. I didn't know which one of them stirred the greater ache in me.

Ben's experience was even grimmer. One hot summer day, Ben and three friends were in a car stopped at a traffic light at one of the busiest intersections in our conservative, middle-class neighborhood. They saw a man, stumbling drunkenly down the sidewalk, stop to urinate into the street. As the other boys pointed and laughed, Ben just said: "That's my dad." He didn't flinch from letting them know he was serious.

That same week, a police car pulled up in front of my house. A serious young officer told me, kindly, hesitantly, "I'm sorry, ma'am, but I have your husband here." "My ex," I said. "Well, he asked to come here.

He's drunk, and he's soiled himself."

Doug sat on my kitchen floor, terrified and ashamed. "I don't know what's happening to me," he cried. I felt only pity and helplessness. I went to find clean clothes for him, but when I got back, he was gone. I drove around the neighborhood for hours, but couldn't find him. It was two days before he showed up again. He had no idea where he'd been.

Doug's family tried to help, and he saw doctors, especially at first. But true assistance was hard to come by. It is nearly, if not completely, impossible to force an adult into treatment. It is particularly difficult if finances are limited.

As he kept up his compulsive routine of walking the streets, heavily inebriated, Doug started to fall down. He was always bruised and bloodied. Scars erased half of one eyebrow. His nose was broken so many times that it nearly formed a circle. He knocked out his front teeth. Not a week went by that I didn't get at least one phone call from the emergency room to come get him.

During one ER visit, a determined social worker managed to get Doug admitted into a 30-day rehab program. At the end of the month, he seemed changed. He immediately phoned bill collectors and began forming a plan to return to work. I was impressed, thrilled. His first night home, he asked me for a ride to an AA meeting. The third night, I dropped him off at the meeting, and as I later learned, he headed straight for the liquor store.

The injuries, the calls from the hospital began again. I begged Doug not to leave his house. I promised to bring groceries and check on his needs daily. The one-time gourmet cook would choke down a frozen dinner. Mostly, he just wanted vodka. And sometimes I delivered that, too—anything to keep him off the streets. Family and friends told me I should let Doug "hit bottom." I was horrified to think it could get worse. They called me an enabler, and they were right. But it was difficult to just walk away from a man I cared about, a man in such desperate need of help. I was deeply conflicted, no matter how much well-intentioned, even expert, advice I received.

One day, at the usual time, I knocked on his door. I heard him on the other side trying to unfasten the lock. Maybe a half a minute passed as he fumbled with the simple latch. Finally, he opened the door. He had dropped to his knees to stabilize himself, and he looked up at me, his eyes sunken into dark holes.

"You're scaring the hell out of me," I said.

"Me, too."

Despite his obvious unsteadiness, he seemed sober. I left for the grocery, telling him, "I'm taking a key." He wasn't in the house when I returned, and I found him lying on the patio. He had a large scrape on the back of his head and had to crawl to get back into the house.

"Why are you out here?" I asked. "What happened?"

"I guess I was drunk," he said. But that didn't seem possible, given that I'd been gone only 20 minutes. And he still sounded sober, if confused.

I tried to take him to the emergency room, but he refused. "I promise I'll go tomorrow," he said. "Just not now." The idea of another trip to the hospital overwhelmed me, too.

I checked on him a few hours later. He wasn't drinking and he seemed comfortable.

"I appreciate what you're trying to do," he told me.

I arrived at 7:30 the next morning and let myself in. Doug wasn't on the couch. Out of the corner of my eye, I glimpsed something on the hallway floor.

It looked like he had just laid down to rest; he was on his back, his arms and legs in a relaxed, natural state. But the dull, half-opened eyes, locked in an eternal stare, told me it was over.

He was 49 years old.

Leah, home from college for summer break, took on the difficult task of notifying family. I made one phone call, to Gary.

Two days later, Gary was at my house. Doug's two exes and three children worked together through our grief to plan a funeral. I think it did justice to his memory, to his life.

LOOKING FOR ANSWERS

The boys couldn't bring themselves to go inside Doug's house again, but Leah helped me box up his things. We glimpsed anew the descent of

Doug's diseased mind. There was the filth and chaos of the living room, where he'd spent his last months—blood and feces on the carpet and furniture, empty vodka bottles under the sofa, stacks and stacks and stacks of unopened mail.

But upstairs, we found memories of the Doug we'd known. There were dozens of framed photos of the children and even one of us on our wedding day. All his beautiful clothes, unworn for many months, were meticulously sorted by color. In his desk were thick folders of complex work projects. There were neatly filled-out workbooks from the French course he'd been taking and an application to a culinary school in New York.

But there was no answer to our question: What happened?

Today, three and a half years after Doug's death, life has gone on. Leah is completing a master's degree in musicology and is applying to Ph.D. programs. Jacob works at a specialty food store and catering company and is considering culinary schools. Ben is a short-order cook by day and a singer/songwriter/keyboardist in a rock band by night.

My mother has long since beaten her cancer. She recently celebrated her 90th birthday by going bowling with her grandchildren and great-grandchildren.

As for me, I continue my editing work, including on this book. I'm in a loving relationship with a wonderful man. He pampers me and pushes me. Under his prodding, I finished writing a novel for middle-graders, a long-time ambition of mine. It will be published in 2010.

When people ask how Doug died, my honest response is: inch by inch. I'm not sure I did anything that helped Doug in those last months. I didn't improve his circumstances; I didn't change the outcome. But without me, he would have been alone. And without me, there would be no one to tell his story. It has helped me to tell it. Where once I saw myself as dependent and weak, I now recognize self-reliance, even strength. But I see that only in retrospect.

My hope is that Doug's story, our story, can help to strip away the shame and secrecy surrounding mental illness and alcoholism. What can't be spoken can't be cured. As the adage goes, we're only as sick as our secrets. This is true of society as well as individuals.

So ask for help and offer it.

Speak up. Speak out.

KACY COOK is a writer and editor in Columbus, Ohio. She is copy editor of *Women on Fire*. Her first children's book will be published by Marshall Cavendish in 2010. The story, which follows the relationship of a girl and a squirrel, is called *Nuts*. She is co-editor, with Arnold Adoff, of *Virginia Hamilton: Speeches, Essays and Conversations*, to be published in 2010 by Scholastic/Blue Sky Press.

Slowing Down the Speed of Life

Learning to do absolutely nothing can bring you everything you've always wanted

 THERESA VOLKMANN

Every time I ran into my friend, Lynne, I would get the feeling she really needed to talk, but we never seemed to find a convenient time to connect. With my husband David out of town today and my son Daniel at school, I decided to invite her to have a mid-morning cup of tea at my house.

Lynne arrived on my front door step at the appointed time, looking the same as usual—well put together and under control.

We did the customary small talk as I moved through the kitchen filling the teapot and putting it on the stove to boil. She told me that her two kids were great, loved their teachers and were doing well in school. Her husband had just received a promotion and was successfully moving up the corporate ladder at his company. Lynne herself was busy volunteering with a local nonprofit and was in the middle of helping to plan their annual gala. Everything in her life seemed to be perfect.

As we moved to the kitchen table and started selecting the flavor of tea to have, I started to notice a little hesitation in her voice. Lynne took her time steeping her tea bag, and seemed to be overly engrossed in the process of getting her tea just right. The period of silence grew, and finally she looked at me with tears welling up in her eyes.

"Everyone thinks everything is perfect in my life," she started. "Everything should be perfect. I have nothing to complain about. Why don't I feel perfect? I'm exhausted, confused and feel like a failure."

THE NEED FOR PERFECTION

My heart ached for her. I remembered those helpless feelings, the doubt, confusion and, most of all, the feelings of being a fraud. They all came flooding back to me. Four years ago on the outside I looked like I had the perfect life, yet on the inside I felt like a failure.

I had to take a deep breath to quash those feelings from overtaking me again. "Do you remember when I broke my ankle four years ago?" I asked. I went on to explain that I had walked in her shoes and felt the same way before I was injured. There was the beginning of a look of relief in Lynne's eyes. I did understand how she felt.

When the doctor told me how serious my injury was and broke the news I would be off my feet for three months, I thought this was the worst thing that could happen to me. Driving a car was out of the picture, so I lost my independence and with it my ability to be everything to everybody.

In hindsight, this accident was the best thing that could have happened to my family and me. I then assured Lynne that she didn't need to be on crutches to learn the lessons I had.

Lynne followed me back to the stove to get more hot water for our tea without saying anything. I knew she was thinking about what I had just confessed. When I had felt the way she was feeling, I thought I was the only one in the world struggling. Everyone around me seemed to be living the perfect life.

Instead of heading back to the kitchen table with our tea, I suggested we move into the living room and get comfortable. On our way to the other room, I grabbed a box of tissues. I was certain we would need them as our conversation progressed.

I could see the wheels turning in Lynne's head as she watched me take off my shoes and snuggle into my favorite chair. How could I say being stuck at home for three months was a blessing? How could she let go of the always-put together façade she had created for herself and share her innermost thoughts with me?

There was a reason Lynne was at my house, and she opened up about her feelings. She was looking for answers, and I hoped I could lead her to them.

I knew the ice needed to be broken, and I noticed Daniel had left one of his little bouncy balls in the living room. As I grabbed the ball I told Lynne, "My life before my broken ankle was exactly like this ball in action." With a hard, quick bounce I set it into motion.

OUT OF CONTROL

The ball took some big bounces and then started to bounce off of everything it hit at odd angles. "See, trying to capture it is very hard. Attempting to control it when it's in motion is almost impossible," I explained, while making a complete fool of myself trying to catch it.

"My busy schedule before my broken ankle was like this ball; it never wanted to stop, and I never knew where my day would end up." I finally caught the ball. "My busy schedule was forced to come to a screeching stop," I said, holding the ball in the palm of my hand.

I once again got comfortable in my favorite chair. "I wondered how everyone around me would survive. The ego blow that came when everyone capably handled all of his or her own problems was huge. I wasn't as important as I thought or hoped I was. My self-worth at that time was tied to my datebook. The more appointments, meetings and events that I had, the more important I was," I confessed to her.

Lynne seemed lost in thought as I continued speaking, "This was the point in my life when I learned I had been so busy being everything to everyone I had forgotten how to take care of myself. I was like this ball, bouncing everywhere and never really being under control."

As the first tear started to roll down Lynne's cheek, I knew my words were hitting home. I handed a tissue to her and added, "All that motion was exhausting."

"Staying home took all the motion and chaos out of my life," I said and placed the ball on the footstool between us. "Sitting home by myself forced me to become reacquainted with someone I hadn't thought about in years—me. I had to learn how to entertain myself. I had to figure out how to be interesting to myself. From this, I learned I'm a pretty cool, fun person."

I knew she needed some time to regroup and to let some of what

I had just said sink in. "How long has it been since you have done absolutely nothing?" I asked. This question caused a little squirm and hesitation from her.

"There is always someone who needs something" was her response.

I sat quietly sipping my tea to give her some more time to think about our conversation. That's when the single tear rolling down her check was joined by others, and the crying started in earnest. "There are so many people and projects demanding time from me that I can't even think about doing something for myself."

"If I even hesitate, they lay on the guilt," she continued. Lynne's life was filled with guilt and exhaustion. How I remembered those painful feelings. Right now she couldn't see her way out of the bouncing ball routine she'd created for herself.

QUIET TIME

"Have you ever noticed how close I park to school in the afternoons?" I asked. "Most people probably think I go early to get the good spot. But do you want to know the real reason?"

With a nod from Lynne, I explained, "The good parking spot is a bonus, but the real reason I go early is to have that extra 15 minutes of quiet time. I don't take my cell phone. I turn off the car and the radio, and I just sit there doing nothing."

"The whole point of doing nothing is just that—you do nothing. Magic things happen when you take the time to do nothing at all. When you are always busy, there's no time to find solutions to your nagging problems. I can't tell you how many times doing nothing has led me to innovative, new and brilliant solutions," I explained to a quiet Lynne.

After a breath, and sitting still for a moment I continued. "Doing nothing let's me feel grateful for all of the great things I have in my life. Doing nothing gives me the time I need to become reacquainted with myself. Instead of just doing things for others, I get to spend some time thinking and dreaming about my hopes and visions for the future."

"That good parking spot is what most people think that I'm after, only a few others know of the magic that happens in that parking spot," I finished.

"Are you ready to spend a few minutes doing nothing?" I asked as I went to the stash of bubbles and wands I always keep handy. Before I met my husband, I had had a stressful job. One day, completely by accident, I discovered that blowing bubbles was a great way to relieve stress. As we walked out the back door with bubbles and wands in our hands, she didn't seem to be trying as hard to look under control.

After a few minutes I heard a quiet murmur, "I needed that." I smiled knowing that Lynne now understood the importance and great feeling of relief that comes from doing nothing.

CREATING AN ILLUSION

As we headed back inside to the kitchen to make a salad for lunch, I mentioned how I felt about perfection before my broken ankle. When I was finding my importance in my datebook, I was attempting to be perfect, or more appropriately said, the illusion of perfection.

Doing the right things, saying the right things and looking just the right way took over my life. The way I appeared was much more important than the way I felt, or who I was on the inside. I may have thought that I looked perfect on the outside, but I always felt inadequate on the inside. The worse I felt on the inside, the more I worked on the outside to look perfect.

It wasn't until I broke my ankle that I realized how much pressure I had been putting on myself, along with the pressure I was putting on everyone around me. I spent so much energy on being the "perfect wife" and the "perfect mom." During this time, I also pressured David and Daniel to put as much energy into being perfect in their roles as I was putting into mine.

Lynne nodded her head. I knew this was what she was experiencing when she walked through my front door this morning. This is what she really came to hear. She had seen my "perfect stage" and had watched my transformation into becoming a "mom on purpose."

I told her how during this time in my life I felt as though everyone else was molding me, bending me, and putting me into positions I couldn't get out of. "Do you remember Gumby, the flexible toy?" I asked.

"You could bend it and pose it in almost any position you wanted. While I was attempting to be perfect, I was allowing others to position me. All the while I was attempting to bend and position David and Daniel as well."

In addition to being disappointed in myself for failing to reach perfection in my roles, I was disappointed in David and Daniel. Not only had I stopped just being myself, I had forgotten who David was and why I had married him. Sadly, I hadn't even started to realize who my little boy was. I only knew how I wanted Daniel to behave.

Getting away from everyone and everything that was pulling me in different directions finally let me realize who I was again. Without all of the outside influences, I got to explore who I was and what was important to me. Once I started to be comfortable with myself, I started to see who David and Daniel really were.

Just then the phone rang. "I love caller ID," I commented as I checked to see who was calling. Only a phone call from Daniel's school or from David would be answered. "Do you want some water while I'm up?" I asked. Looking back at Lynne, I could see her eyes were a little brighter, her smile a little bigger, and her shoulders looked more relaxed. A few moments of quiet were going to be good for her. I wanted her to think for a little while about all she had heard.

GIVING UP CONTROL

I ducked into my office to get the next item I wanted to talk to her about: my Magic Eight Ball. After suggesting we return to the living room, I handed a bottle of water to Lynne and sat the Magic Eight Ball on the footstool between us. She didn't look surprised when I came out with something different. She was totally open to learning something new.

"When I was getting my importance from my datebook, I was attempting to be perfect for everyone," I started. "I thought perfection was doing what others wanted and expected me to do. I couldn't do that without asking them what they thought, and what they wanted. Bit by bit I was turning over more and more of my life to other people's control."

With this statement I saw Lynne's eyes darken and her shoulders become tense again. "At first no one said anything until I asked for their input." Then I started to tell her about how the people around me stopped waiting to give me their thoughts, and just told me what to do without my asking. Finally, several of these individuals felt they held so much power in my life that they would tell me what I should do and then got angry if I didn't do it.

During my time stuck at home, I started to realize how much control of my life I had turned over to the people around me. As I got more and more comfortable with who I was, I also started to discover who David and Daniel were. That's when I developed my three truths that I live by today:

1. No one knows me as well as I do. I know what is right and wrong for me in my life.
2. No one knows David the way that I do. I know what is right and wrong for our relationship and our partnership in parenting.
3. No one knows Daniel the way that I do. It's up to David and I to decide what is right and wrong for our son.

That's when I picked up the Magic Eight Ball and handed it to Lynne. I explained, "When you ask other people what you should do, they don't know your situation the way that you do. When they give you advice, they are giving it based on the information that they know. The advice you get from them is no better than the advice you would get from a Magic Eight Ball."

Lynne's eyes brightened and shoulders relaxed again as I told her that now when I get the urge to ask someone what I should do, I ask the Eight Ball instead. At least it doesn't suffer from hurt feelings if I don't follow it.

A glance at the clock told me our day together had to come to an end. It was time for me to drive to school, get my great parking spot, and enjoy doing nothing.

"Do you remember how hard it was for me to keep up with the bouncing ball?" I asked Lynne. "If you set your priorities and keep to them, you'll slow down the speed of life." I slowly dropped the ball and then caught it. "If you stop asking everyone what you should do and follow your heart, you'll slow down the speed of life."

I dropped the ball again. "Doing nothing and letting the magic happen is the key to doing this." I caught the ball.

With her eyes clear and shoulders relaxed, Lynne no longer looked like a woman attempting to hold everything together. When we hugged at the front door, I handed the bouncy ball to her as a reminder to slow down the speed of her life.

As she drove away, I knew a very different mom would be picking her kids up from school today.

Most of the time, **THERESA VOLKMANN** can be found with her husband David and son Daniel in Northern Nevada. She's the founder of You on Purpose, where she encourages you to "slow down the speed of life", and start to design a life that is "tailor-made" just for you! You can listen to her weekly radio show, and sign up for her weekly email newsletter at YouOnPurpose.com.

Stepping Off of the Corporate Ladder

How one workaholic made a 180-degree turn, quit her job and moved to balance her life

ALLISON BARRY

At age 41 it hit me. I woke one morning from a work-induced "coma" and started to wonder: Who is this slightly cranky workaholic I've become? What do I really want in life? Does my career make me happy? What about my dream of marriage and children?

Even though I had a great job and was at the top of my game, collecting awards and making good money, it wasn't enough. For years, I had struggled to find a balance between the personal and professional sides of my life. But every time I tried to make the needed changes, I became overwhelmed. I talked myself in circles and just kept slipping back into the same old rut. How did I get into this state? When had I established a pattern of letting my work become my life?

My career was in software. I started out working in customer support, as a manager of many with a never-ending to-do list. Then one night at a wedding reception, a friend yelled across the room, "How'd you like to make $100,000 a year?" She recruited me into sales. Once I got the hang of it, I found that I was pretty good at it, and I even learned to love it. I was living in Boston, but I soon became intimately familiar with life on the road, as most of our business was in the New York/New Jersey area.

After years of commuting and watching my social life dwindle to virtually nothing, something had to give. I decided to move to New Jersey to simplify my life.

But things did not get simpler. A series of work transitions came in rapid succession: Only a year later, I left my job to work for a small startup company, which was then purchased by a larger corporation. The next year, I left that job to work with former co-workers, this time in marketing. But, within months, I realized that position was not a good fit for me either. To make matters worse, at about the same time, I finally ended (or we ended—I can't remember) a long on-again, off-again relationship.

It felt like a good time to stop and reassess.

I wanted to take a step back and focus on regaining control of my life and health. So I decided to take a three-month sabbatical. And even though I had no new prospects on the horizon, I quit my job.

It was a big step toward change. Finally. But only six weeks later, I began backsliding. I went on a job interview, and it was amazing. The job seemed designed for me. What else could I do? I quickly accepted the offer to work at a hot Internet startup company.

I got right back onto the rollercoaster.

THE PROFESSIONAL RIDE OF MY LIFE

It seemed that all those previous jobs and struggles were only preparing me for this new position. It's hard to describe the excitement and energy at the company. In 1999, the promise of "going public" and riding the Internet stock wave was bringing the best-of-the-best people to this company. I was working with the most motivated and talented group in the business. It was exhilarating! Software sales is a male-dominated profession, but I was determined to make my mark and be taken seriously. I decided that I was going to be a "rock star" at this company. I knew I had all the skills and the background to do it. It became my motto that I would never lose a deal because I didn't work hard enough. The rocket ship took off. We went public the summer of 1999 and had a successful IPO (initial public offering), and it just so happened that we had a great product. People would actually lean forward with their mouths hanging open when I would demonstrate the functionality. This job was fun! We often worked well into the night and on weekends, including one all-day Saturday presentation—whatever it took. My first year I helped to sell lots of software, and I was one of the top three producers in the company. That became my new goal: to be one of the top three producers every year. It was my mission and focus.

When I took the job, my going-in plan had been to work hard, reap the rewards of the stock craze and re-evaluate in four years, after I was fully vested and could sell all my stock. At that point I would be 39, hopefully financially set for life, in a relationship or perhaps even married, and ready to finally make a change, one that would focus on me and my needs.

Well, some time in the first quarter of 2001, the Internet bubble popped. We were a front-page story of a "dot com" that turned into a "dot bomb." The stock plummeted and then came the downsizing. The company did finally settle down, and the sales were still there. I continued to make that goal of being a top-three performer. I had set my standards and established myself as a well-prepared, detail-oriented, competitive and dedicated soldier. Who could step back from that? My professional self-esteem was at an all-time high.

But what about the rest of my life?

Those four years passed quickly, and it was time for my re-evaluation. I was turning 40, and the last of my closest single friends was about to head down the aisle. I felt that life was passing me by as I prepared for my demos, collected my awards and shopped on weekends to help fill the void. I looked at those other things my friends had, the things I used to dream about—marriage and a family. I often thought, "I need to find a man." I did date from time to time, but I made no room in my life or in my heart for someone special.

So what about my dream of having children? My biological clock was ticking. I thought about adoption or going to "the bank." I bought books, joined an Internet chat group and tried to muster the courage to move forward with either option. But that led to another spiral. I didn't have the network or support I felt I needed in New Jersey to be a single mom. I would have to move back to Boston, and then I would be right back where I started, traveling all the time, with no time for a child and no life. Yet if I didn't do this job, what would I do? How could I figure that out and have a baby at the same time? What should I do first? What's keeping me from having a relationship? Do you have a headache yet? This was the quagmire within my head. I needed help!

GETTING CLARITY AND CREATING A PLAN

Perhaps more than anything, I wanted to find my passion again. I wanted to feel fervor about something other than my commission checks. I told a good friend of my unhappiness and inability to move forward. "Can you afford to take a year off?" she asked. I said that I could. "Then why don't you? You may never get a chance like this again." What a revelation!

My fabulous friend also gave me a gift of a coaching session with Debbie Phillips. Within the first hour on the phone, I knew that this was just what I needed: a supportive coach to help me sift through the noise in my head and make a plan. I jumped further into the process with Debbie by having a "Vision Day," which is her strategic planning day for your life. I've had three so far, and they have played an important role in the planning and execution of my transition, my road to self-discovery.

Debbie and her husband and fellow life coach, Rob Berkley, got me to open up. I was a bit nervous at first, as I had never spent a whole day talking about me, and there are areas about myself that I don't discuss easily. In a supportive and welcoming environment, they mixed patience and lots of great questions to help me develop a deeper awareness of myself. I began to appreciate my accomplishments and to recognize my priorities. I learned the importance of breaking down big ideas, dreams and roadblocks into small doable steps. We put the wheels in motion for major changes.

First, I had to get out of the software business. I had lost my passion for my once beloved job. I wasn't sure if it would be a permanent departure, but I had to leave. With this decision, a weight lifted. I felt energetic, motivated and the most optimistic I had felt in a long time.

I also knew that I wanted to be back in Boston, where my family and closest friends live. New Jersey had been great for my career, but Boston was home.

I had my plan mapped out in my head: I would quit my job, move to Boston and rent an apartment in the city. I would take a year off and focus on my health, my love life and finding my passion. It took just over a year to execute this plan. Delivery of commissions became the driver of my timeline, and I ended up adjusting my move date a couple of times as payouts were delayed. I am proud to say that I did end my last full year of sales as the top performer. It was important to me to leave the company and the people who'd been so good to me on a positive note. I wanted to go without burning my bridges, or even leaving them smoldering.

TRANSITIONING

Finally I was in my cute city apartment, with no particular place to be, and only a few emails every day. All that stress, all that planning and all those projects were behind me. Initially, I had moments of euphoria with the realization that I could just go for a walk for an hour and I could sleep until…whenever. But I also had plenty of moments of anxiety with the realization that no one needed me. I compulsively checked my email for the first two months. I enthusiastically decorated my small apartment, making projects out of the few things that needed to be done.

I took some time at Cape Cod that summer. With friends streaming in and out, I was finally settling in to a more relaxed existence. Fall brought a family trip to France—some time in Paris with my sister and a week in a villa in Provence. The moments of euphoria far out-weighed the freak-outs.I settled into a new life and daily routine in Boston. I had eaten my way through the stress and the general three-month celebration of my new freedom, and I was ready to work on my health. I made my physical well-being and the gym my new "job." Workouts, often followed by naps and periodic massages, became my daily routine. If it sounds great…well, it was!

FIND A WAY TO GIVE BACK

But then I discovered another step to reclaiming my passion and finding balance in my life: volunteering. Like most people, I have a desire to give back and to help others. There truly is nothing like the feeling of knowing you've made a difference in someone else's life.

I also had a desire to shake up my routine and get out of my comfort zone (within reason, of course. I'm not ready for shark-cage diving yet) in hopes of finding that "aha!" moment when I would know my true calling. With that in mind, my first volunteer adventure took me to New Orleans in the aftermath of Hurricane Katrina. I didn't know any of my 30 fellow volunteers, but I hoped to make connections, expand my horizons and feel inspired. It was all that and more. We stayed with 70 other volunteers in a church annex for a week, something that was definitely outside my comfort zone. But not only did I survive the bunkhouse setup, I also quickly fell in love with my volunteer group. A subset of this group has become a new circle of friends, a source of inspiration and joy. We get together regularly to share our triumphs and frustrations. I am proud to have been part of this intense and inspirational experience. Each day we signed up for projects, and I gravitated toward community service. One day we put on an Earth Day fair for a local school in a crime-ridden neighborhood. As the kids came running to our arts-and-crafts table and the chaos began, one of the little girls just climbed into my lap without asking. I could feel her need for love and affection, and I hoped that I helped for those few minutes. I wished I could take her with me. It was humbling, exhausting and inspiring, and it reminded me how much I enjoy children and how much need there is for love.

My second big volunteer adventure was truly a trip of a lifetime. Similar to New Orleans, I was in search of a volunteer vacation. I thought this was a great way to visit a part of the world I might not see otherwise and a great way to do it alone. Some of my volunteer friends had told me about Earthwatch, a not-for-profit organization that helps to staff eco-friendly projects around the globe with volunteers. I had thoughts of Asia and Africa, two continents I'd never seen. I checked out the expeditions on the group's website, clicked on Africa and one of the first ones I saw was "Saving the Cheetah." Loving cats, I was immediately drawn to this project: two weeks in the middle of Namibia, helping to save the wild cheetah. How cool! I even talked a good friend into coming with me. Again, I was placed outside my comfort zone. Even though I didn't know what to expect, I was blown away by my own reaction: I was giddy. I could not stop giggling! I had not been that happy since, well, since

I don't remember when. For two weeks I was just a volunteer, in the middle of the African bush, making sure I fed the cheetahs right, didn't get bitten by a snake, and that I made it to my assigned tasks on time. I wasn't the single unemployed woman worrying about everything. I was part of a mission and seeing incredible animals and nature every day.

My friend and I even extended our two weeks in Namibia to include a safari and a few days in Capetown, South Africa. The safari was equally as intoxicating. Being four feet from a huge lion certainly changes one's perspective. I never thought of myself as a "nature gal," but my three weeks in the African bush were peaceful and humbling for me. The people and the animals touched my heart, and I realized I need more of that in my life. I know I will return to the cheetah farm and for more safaris. I now include Africa in my thoughts of future adventures and volunteering.

RESULTS AND NEXT STEPS

I have started joking that what was once my one-year sabbatical is instead my five-year plan. I did have a little anxiety when I passed that one-year mark. Suddenly I was frequently being asked what I was going to do, and when was I going back to work. I started to listen, thinking that I should know this by now. But one of the unexpected benefits of a more relaxed life is being much more in tune with my thoughts and feelings. I quickly realized that I wasn't ready to jump into anything. And that was OK.

Having time to think about my feelings and listen to my body has been amazing. I've been able to get into my own sleeping rhythm (which just confirmed that I'm not an early morning fan), get the rest I need, exercise to feel strong and healthy again, and develop the awareness to keep that negative voice in my head in check—most of the time.

I have no regrets. I haven't been disappointed for a second by making any of these changes. I also know that my time at the startup company was meant to be. The benefits for me, both financially and professionally, cannot be measured. I left with nothing on the table, and I am eternally grateful for everything that has led to this time during which I have the resources and support to take such a long break.

I am now two and a half years into my transition. I admit that I still have ups and downs as I weigh my love of free time, taking classes and traveling with the recent economic downturn and its impact on my finances. Whatever I do next, I go into it with a new self-awareness, a focus on my health and a need to maintain balance.

As for the process and transition, having firm goals and a general plan to rely on was critical for me. Although I had to work out the details along the way, and it seemed as if it would take forever, it was much easier with a vision and end goal. I am determined to follow my passion, and to maintain a work/life balance in the future. I will find that man, discover that career of passion and live my fullest life!

ALLISON BARRY resides outside of Boston, Mass. She has a bachelor of science in computer science and applied mathematics from Union College, and held a variety of positions in the software industry for 21 years, spanning customer hotline support, management, marketing and sales. She enjoys spending time with family and friends, traveling, and Cape Cod. She is currently enjoying the search for passion in a new career and a romantic relationship. She can be reached at abarry23@yahoo.com.

Learning to Let Go...
to Live

My Divorce: the struggle that gave me a new beginning

ANDREA DOWDING

I remember the moment I decided to end my marriage.

I was relieved and sick to my stomach, calm and frightened, all at the same time. But in that instant, my resolve finally out-weighed the excruciating back and forth—letting go and holding on—that had characterized the eight-year process of making the decision.

I was in the local drugstore searching for cold remedies when I knew that I could no longer be joined to this man in spirit, name or by law. In the car on the way to the pharmacy, we had engaged in yet another mostly one-sided conversation about our finances, our family and our future. I was looking for middle ground, but there was only distance. Worse, there was blame and ridicule.

It was time. My daughters were 2, 3 and 7 at the time.

ONCE UPON A TIME

My first husband and I married young. He was a full-time college student, and I worked three jobs to support the family. Days, I was an optician in the ophthalmology clinic at a large state university; evenings, I worked in a small eyeglass boutique; and weekends I was a phlebotomist at a local hospital. In a common scenario, our master plan was that I would complete my degree when my husband had finished his.

After graduation, my husband took a job teaching health at a private

Christian school. The school was the brainchild of a committee made up of well-intentioned and dedicated former public school educators and members of large congregation we were familiar with. The pay was low and the health benefits were not competitive. In addition to his classroom responsibilities, my husband also served as the athletic director as well as the soccer and the basketball coach for a small added stipend. Finances were challenging, and I continued to work until our first daughter, Betsy, was born, putting my college plans on hold once more.

Over the next five years, I gave birth to two more beautiful daughters. Betsy was four when Kellie Diane was born, and Kellie was 14 months when Abby arrived. I wanted so much for each of them, but mostly I wanted to provide a foundation of experiences and awareness that would translate to future opportunity and healthy self-esteem. I wanted to give my girls opportunities that would expand their experiences and expose them to new environments and ideas. But the financial reality of our situation was a problem.

HAVE A LITTLE FAITH

I couldn't even bring up the subject of money without it turning to the apparent lack of faith on my part. At times the school administrators echoed this sentiment to me, even in group settings. In one conversation, a female administrator shared in the most helpful way she could that maybe I best not even "window shop as it might be a source of temptation to spend." This was strange advice, as most of my shopping was done at second-hand shops, garage sales and through store layaway plans.

I had an incredible love of and affinity for family life, but I did not subscribe to the traditional belief of submissive behavior. I believed that a woman's talents could not only benefit her home and church community, but also could be highlighted in leadership positions in the business world. And I believed that men and women had a responsibility to cultivate their gifts. Wealth and abundance were available to everyone and could be used as vehicles for doing good things and changing lives in positive ways.

As our beliefs became more antithetical, the silence and chastisement became more intense. If I didn't respond in the proper way or if my spirit of independence became too amplified, my husband and I didn't speak at all.

I was constantly torn between my apparent "lack of faith" in failing to accept the status quo and my life experience of how goal setting and a strong work ethic could change current reality. My father had been self-employed and started his own insurance agency when his four children were in middle school. While supporting us on commissions, my parents always found a way to more than make ends meet and were role models in a demonstrating a "can do" attitude to create success.

NECESSITY IS THE MOTHER OF INVENTION

I started a home business from my kitchen table when Betsy was two. I put together a collection of better home goods and hand-painted folk art pieces to sell, Tupperware style through home parties. I named my enterprise Sweet Betsy after my daughter. As I developed the business, I was able to keep Betsy's needs as my priority by booking home shows at night. This also helped to minimize child-care costs.

As with many women who have been in traditional roles, I found that building a small business could provide an unparalleled opportunity for personal growth. I had no cash to start up the business, so I took the first pieces on consignment and built up cash reserves to begin to find better artists and buy sales samples. I found that the easiest and most inexpensive way to get started in business in the 1980s was the direct-selling model of home shows. Payment for goods was received the night of the show. The cash flow was what our family needed, but little did I know that the contact with women in their homes was to become my lifeline. I had healthy conversation, validation and purpose through my business, and soon that became my journey to discover my greater self.

DISCOVERING MY STRENGTHS

Inventory was negligible in the beginning because I developed a custom made-to-order and personalized line of products in addition to the consignment products that I offered. Not necessarily a strategic plan, but born out of financial necessity, this approach of customized products was the sure thing that helped my business grow that first year. I had developed a niche.

I loved developing the products for Sweet Betsy home shows. When I was working with the artists and crafters who were creating my small line of goods, I began to tap into a wellspring of personal creativity that I was unaware that I had. I found joy and comfort in this new world. I was learning about new methods of making products and how to look for new trends at a grass-roots level. I became keenly aware of color palettes and font styles.

I learned to ask my customers key questions about what they were looking for and how they were planning on using the products they purchased. This would be my foundation and stepping stone to my future position as executive director of product innovation for a billion-dollar company and co-author of 27 U.S. patents in product design!

I was protective of those conversations and the new world that I was building. I would normally do all my creative work during the day. After I took Betsy to the bus stop each morning, I'd pack the babies into the car and go to see my artists and suppliers. My days transformed into private periods of growth and respite (even though hectic, with two in diapers). I found a new strength in relationships outside the confines of my marriage and the church.

As Sweet Betsy grew and gained a following, my company's reputation for quality goods grew as well. I had women approach me about selling Sweet Betsy products. I was flattered and panicked at the same time. I had no idea how to set the financial structure or compensation plan. I didn't have a training program or a recognition plan in place (I certainly could have used Women on Fire back then).

The women who approached me wanted to join Sweet Betsy for a number of reasons. Some needed extra income but wanted to be home with their children, some needed a creative outlet, and some were simply looking for something to call their own. I knew it was the right decision to open up my doors, even though I didn't have the infrastructure in place to support the kind of growth that they would bring. The women that became part of the business were remarkable. They were talented and helpful and offered unconditional support. I am eternally grateful for these brilliant women that gave me more than I could have ever offered them.

I began to feel the distinction between healthy and unhealthy relationship as I experienced the different family dynamics in the homes I visited several nights a week. My sense of self stirred, and I started to draw distinctions between what I could and couldn't tolerate. My business built out of financial necessity had become my safety net and lifeline. Even though I didn't realize it at the time, I knew that it somehow served me in a larger way.

I HEARD MY OWN VOICE

I had kept many things to myself over the years. I had been isolated and alone. Now I reached out to my family, and this time I was specific in my conversations. My sister, Jennifer, drove with me to my first visit with an attorney to begin the divorce process. She later told me that she had never seen me in such a fragile state and that I was almost unrecognizable in spirit.

My family and a few childhood friends proved to be a remarkable source of encouragement. I like to call these dear family members and friends my nuclear support system—small but very powerful, pure in spirit and authentic in intent. There is support and transformational change in purity and authenticity. I learned a lot about authentic communities vs. superficial support systems during this time, lessons that have served me well.

The thing I most regret is traveling most of that journey alone, without asking for the help I needed. As I became more isolated from a healthy support system, I nearly lost my ability to be clear and articulate about specific situations that weren't tolerable. Establishing healthy personal boundaries was almost nonexistent. I had a hard time letting go of the notion that, because I stayed, I had to accept everything that came my way.

I had a difficult time understanding that no matter how loud the voices were around me, it was *my* voice that needed to resonate above the others and find its way to God. Once I truly believed that my voice was as important to God and his entire magnificent universe as the school administrators' or my husband's, my life began to transform.

During the process of my divorce, I received an unexpected call from an executive of a vibrant new direct-selling company that was just on the brink of exploding. The company was nestled in a small village near my home. I had put together my first Sweet Betsy full-color, four-page brochure, and it had made its way to the office of a vice president of this company. The gentleman had asked me to come for an interview if I had an interest.

I had every intention of growing my small company and was in the process of talking to a woman I planned to ask to become a partner in an effort to increase sales. I had no intention of leaving my home, my business and my nuclear support system to join this company. But at the prompting of my father, who had known the joy and struggle of raising and supporting a family while building and operating a family-owned business, I went for the interview. I came away intrigued but dug my heels in even further. I wasn't budging. I would make it on my own and grow my small business.

I stopped by my father's office on the way home from the interview and we had a long talk. He even pulled out the old T-chart, mapping out the pros and the cons of taking the job.

My father was insightful and told me a story of safety, loyalty and hope. He explained that sometimes the very thing that gets you to a place of safety and happiness (like my Sweet Betsy business) can become the very thing that holds you back when it is time to move on and let go. Here's how the story goes:

TAKE THE CANOE OFF YOUR HEAD

A young native girl, daughter of the village chief, stood on the desolate bank of a raging river and looked across to the opposite bank. She saw a land of opportunity and abundance. Wanting to cross the dangerous water to share in that bounty but not knowing how, she sat dejectedly on the trunk of a giant redwood tree that had been felled by a storm. She began carving images on the tree trunk and marveled at how the redwood enhanced the symbols she carved.

She had seen an image of strange vessels in her dreams and realized the redwood held the key to her future. She began to scoop out the inside of the tree, working feverishly for many days and nights. As her creation took shape, she marveled at the unique life-force of the vessel. Once completed, it became a canoe, covered with symbols of protection and strength. It was both beautiful and fearsome.

The girl entered the raging river, never losing faith in the power of the canoe. After many hardships, she reached the opposite bank and gave thanks to the canoe for its power. As she embraced her new world of opportunity, she carried the canoe on her head everywhere she went. Her new friends marveled at the beauty of the canoe and loved to hear stories of its magical ability to tame the angry river. She prospered, but as time went on, she grew weary of carrying the canoe, and people tired of her story.

The weariness prevented her from exploring new opportunities and became a burden that weighed her down, both in body and spirit. Her heart told her the canoe had served its purpose and that it would always have a place in her life, but it could not be carried into the future. She laid the canoe down with tears in her eyes and walked forward, looking for the next vessel that would propel her into joy and opportunity.

My business, Sweet Betsy, had been a sacred canoe, but it was time to move on and leave it behind for my new opportunity.

Until Dad died, he could always say to me, "Andi, I think there's a canoe on your head," and I would know what he meant. I would know what to do.

P.S. THE REST OF THE STORY

I took the canoe off my head and took the job that Dad and I talked about. A single mother now, the girls and I moved to that quaint little village. I worked my way up in that vibrant, young company that had been on the brink of exploding. I held positions ranging from director of product diversification to executive director of product innovation and ultimately vice president of sales.

The company grew from a $90 million company to a billion-dollar company in just 11 years. It proved to be the ride of a lifetime. I was afforded amazing experiences and opportunities that I could never have even imagined as I sat at my kitchen table creating my small Sweet Betsy business.

Betsy, Kellie and Abby have all traveled extensively, and are (or soon will be) college graduates. They have developed their own unique voices and a sense of style, independence and confidence that serves them well. I am remarried to a wonderful man, and together we added a beautiful daughter (our bonus baby), Mollie, to our blended family of six daughters. Life is good!

The process of knowing when it's time to let go is so difficult for so many of us. I have worked with hundreds of women making transitions, some small, some life changing. The barrier for most revolves around the emotion and difficulty of knowing where and how to start the process. Unnecessary loyalty and guilt, lack of confidence, and courage and prevailing feelings that somehow "I don't deserve it" come into play. As a result, many women may stay in an unhealthy situations or perpetuate unhealthy life patterns far too long and endure far too much damage and pain.

I am grateful for my journey as I have gleaned three important strategies that I use and share on regular basis when starting the process of letting go.

1. I will hear my voice above all others.

2. I will take the canoe off my head when needed.

3. I will surround myself with my nuclear support system.

P.S.S. A NEW DEVELOPMENT

About two years ago, after a successful 16-year run, I lost my job. It was time. It had become a canoe that I hadn't taken off of my head. Within 24 hours, I received this beautiful note from Abby, my 18-year-old college freshman. I think Abby has found her voice!

Dear Mom,

NO WORRIES! You haven't lost anything. You still have a warm home, your health, a family and support system and, most important, you still have God's hand to hold. Take this opportunity to organize your life and make your dreams come true! I highly encourage taking random drives in your car jamming to your music, possibly Meredith Brooke's song "I'm a Bitch!" What is a better remedy?

I will pray for you and everything you bless. I know that God has an incredible plan for you. The possibilities are endless. Maintain confidence, Mom, and don't lose sight of what is an important plan for you. You are the author of the story of your life. This is an amazing duty to have. I have no doubts about your succeeding. It is in your blood; it is part of you.

Don't limit yourself. Barriers aren't necessary. Just take a deep breath and spread your wings. Don't look back. Chances are that you will end up doing something GREAT! If you are hurting right now, try channeling your pain through helping others. You are better at easing other people's pain than you think. Test yourself and discover your hidden passions.

I am here for you. I love you!
Your daughter and friend,
Abby

I look back today. I am blessed.

ANDREA DOWDING is a leader in the innovative field of executive and life coaching, specializing in supporting professional women. She is an accomplished keynote speaker and workshop facilitator, and is currently partnering with Debbie Phillips to extend the Women on Fire™ organization to women around the world through tea parties, workshops and coaching groups. Andrea resides in Dresden, Ohio, with her husband David and three of their six daughters.

PART THREE

Struggling in the Sandwich Generation

Finding the gifts buried deep in the mayo

NATALIE SHOPE GRIFFIN

"They need our permission to operate. The doctors say there is only a 5 percent chance that Mom will survive, and if she does, it's likely she'll be paralyzed or brain dead. I still think we should do the surgery. What do you think?"

As I listened to my brother, my stomach tightened and my throat clenched. "Do it," I said. My husband, Ryan, and I began the trek from Columbus, Ohio, to Bethany Beach, Del., hoping Mom would make it through the night.

My mind replayed the tumultuous relationship I had with my mother, beginning with my first breath. I was born six weeks early and was a "blue baby." But my being born at all seemed a miracle. My brother, Don, had been born 11 years earlier, and then my mother endured nine miscarriages before having me. On her deathbed, my Irish grandmother told my mother she would have a daughter. Almost a year to the day later, there I was, fighting for life.

During my first weeks, I was in neo-natal intensive care with no human touch. I was dying. And Mom was dying from an undiagnosed complication from my birth. After two months, a nurse sneaked me into my mother's room in the middle of the night. Mom hugged me against her skin and I finally ate. She, too, was miraculously revived.

Now, she again lay in a hospital fighting for life. I thought that, maybe, when I got there and took her hand, it would be enough to pull her through.

Mom had had an aortic aneurism. During the ambulance ride to the hospital, she "coded" twice. She had to be packed on ice to stop the blood flow for about 45 minutes while they worked to repair the aorta. Her prospects were not good.

I didn't even know what to hope for, what to pray for. For her to die peacefully? To be miraculously saved? My mind splintered between her life and mine. They had always been so dependent on one another.

After surgery, we held our collective breath as the surgeon tested Mom's ability to move. She could. And just before he started checking her mental faculties, she looked at my husband and said, "Ryan! How is your MBA going?"

Twenty-four hours later, her temperature spiked to 104. She spent 40 fevered days on a ventilator.

COPING WITH TRANSITIONS

During that time, back in Ohio, I gave birth to my first child, Keller. I needed to share my joy, but my father had died eight years earlier, before he ever got to walk me down the aisle, and my mother was wrestling demons in a fevered sleep in Virginia. Bitterness at life's dealings welled up in my throat. This was supposed to be the happiest day of my life. Right?

Keller, my *big*, healthy, bouncing baby boy, was hungry all the time. With each feeding, I felt my own life force drain as I slipped into postpartum depression. I had run my own business for two years, and this would have been my biggest year yet. I missed my tailored black suits and having cocktails with clients. I wanted my life back.

Mom finally came out of the fever, and I took my son to visit her. Through strained vocal cords, she croaked out that she had had a dream: "Dad was there, and I wanted to go with him. But he said, 'Now is not your time, Nancy. You have to go back because of Natalie.'" Those words haunted me for years.

Mom spent a year in Virginia with my brother's family. Somehow, he and his family managed the chaos to get her strong enough to live on her own again. But after a few months without their support, she started

to decline. Even as I was battling with the decision of what to do next, one of Mom's friends called me. "You have to do something," she said. "Nancy is depressed and lonely. She fell the other day and couldn't get to the phone. She needs you."

"I know, I know," I thought, grinding my teeth as I zoomed to the office. I was running late.

Minutes later Mom called. "I just wanted to hear your voice. How is Keller?"

I had a huge sales meeting in a few minutes and needed the time in the car to prepare. "Keller is fine, but I have a meeting. Can I talk to you later?"

Silence. Sniffles.

"I'm sorry. I'm just stressed. How are you? Teri said you fell," I said, merging onto the highway.

"I'm fine!" she tried to convince me. "I just fell trying to clean the bathtub. I have a bruise on my face. That's all."

"Why are you cleaning the bathtub? That's why we hired Shawna!" I pulled into my parking space.

Now she was sobbing. I could see her—from 500 miles away—that open mouth without sound, head raised to the heavens looking for mercy or help.

It felt like a flare gun went off in my stomach. What could I do from Ohio, for godsake?! She wasn't following her doctor's recovery plan. It was her choice, her problem. I somehow composed myself. Cool and business like, I said, "Mom, listen, we'll figure it out." I walked into our conference room, where my new clients were standing. I motioned "one more minute" with the biggest I-have-it-all-together smile I could muster. "Bye, mom. I'll call later."

I apologized for being on the phone and then realized my clients were putting on their coats. Our meeting was to have started a half-hour earlier. They promised to reschedule, but they were peeved that I hadn't even called to say I'd be late.

My business partner shut the door. "How could you do that? We had no idea who these people were or when you would be here. We're selling leadership workshops and, if you can't even be here when you say you will, you don't look like much of a leader."

"My mother!" I said angrily. "She calls me crying…her friends call me pleading…. Keller was up at 4 a.m. But don't worry, I have two more sales calls today. We'll make our goal for the month."

That night, after talking to my mother twice more, the phone rang again. I thought it might be my husband, who was overseas. It was Mom.

"How are you?"

"Mom, you know how I am! I just talked with you two hours ago!" I yelled so loudly that the dog started barking and Keller started crying. "It's just hard for me with you and Don so far away," Mom sobbed. "And I miss your dad."

I was looking for a pane of glass to shove my head through when out of my mouth came the words, "There are options. You could go into assisted living. Or we could buy a big house, and you could move in with us." What?! Where was that glass? It would have been a better choice. But it was too late. The sound of her hopes lifting was deafening.

DISAPPOINTMENT IN UTOPIA

I had unlocked Pandora's box. My husband and brother were irate. Don told me I had to call her back and fix it fast because Mom had started to pack. I fought with myself for days. Maybe I could do it. Maybe I should do it. If anyone could save Mom from her sadness, it would be me, the eternally happy and strong daughter.

I dreamt of being in a boat. I could hear crying all around me, like the sea was made of all the world's tears. The swells were getting larger, like a storm was coming. I capsized in the waves and was pulled underwater. There was my mother's face and the faces of many unknown souls. I tried to swim, but I couldn't escape. We all became entangled and drowned. I woke sweating and gasping for air. I was shaken deeply. Perhaps not even by the dream so much as the deep sadness I had begun to notice.

I finally told Mom that I couldn't take care of her in my home, but I would be happy if she was in an assisted-living facility near me.

Mom moved into assisted living down the street, and I thought I had it made. Assisted living looks fantastic in the brochures—"gray

hairs" playing bocce or cards and laughing with a glass of wine in hand. I thought "they" would look after her, and I could cruise in and out as the cheery daughter. But once she was moved in, I found reality was startlingly different.

For example, I decided to have a "doctor day." I made my son's one-year checkup and an appointment for my mother on the same day so I wouldn't have to take more time off of work. After a day of getting in and out of cars, in and out of doors, and in and out of bathroom stalls with two bags, a baby carrier, a walker and a teetery mother, I was in and out of sanity.

Another day, Mom called in tears because the nurse was three hours late with her medicine. I was so angry with that nurse for messing up my plans for Assisted Living Utopia. I called the nurse manager in a fit of rage. She told me something that brought my agitated state almost to a breaking point.

"Your mom is used to taking Xanax twice as often as she should. She has been overmedicated and is a bit addicted to the drug. You have to explain this to her. She thinks the nurse is out to get her. I'm sorry."

I'm sorry? What kind of thing was that to say? (A) You don't know me well enough to say you're sorry, and (B) don't ever talk about my mother like that! She wouldn't do that in a million years! As soon as I arrived, I saw my mother in her wheelchair reaching for the nurse's sleeve. I crumpled into a chair behind a plastic plant and sobbed. I had failed. I had not moved my mother to Utopia. I had moved her to hell.

In an effort to make the most of things, I took Mom out for lunch. I realized how much her abilities had declined. She couldn't eat, drink or even speak audibly anymore. We sat smiling at each other, pretending everything was the same. I suddenly burst into tears. Mom reached across the table, held my hand and said, "I wish I would just go, so you wouldn't have to suffer." I almost choked on my heart as it broke.

I didn't talk to anyone about mom for weeks after this. I hadn't even talked to my husband in *months*. Ryan was absorbed in completing his MBA, which included two-week trips overseas every six weeks and homework and conference calls every night. He buried himself in his books so he wouldn't have to deal with this fire-breathing, weepy wife. Other than transactional exchanges, we had had only one night out when it felt like old times.

I had to talk to Ryan or I thought I might die from the weight in my chest. Then I couldn't stop crying. I joked that maybe I was pregnant, which I thought was hilarious as we had had sex only twice in the last seven months. He didn't laugh. He raced out and bought a pregnancy test. It was positive.

I was overwhelmed. I could almost visualize the light of my soul being sucked into the baby, the only bright spot inside me. As she grew brighter—and thankfully she did—I grew more despondent. Part of me wished I were pregnant with triplets so someone would order me to take care of myself. I could quit taking crazy phone calls from my mother, faking enthusiasm in leadership workshops and cleaning baby vomit out of my cashmere sweaters.

When Kaia was born, she didn't make a peep, but her eyes were as bright as the stars. With her peaceful and easy arrival, some internal peace was restored to my system.

Just before I gave birth to Kaia, my mother fell—while standing on a chair to fix a curtain—and broke her hip. After surgery, she went into a nursing home. She never made it out. My children and I visited three or four times a week for more than a year in an effort to keep her spirits lifted. She was so sad, and I was so sad.

As Mom's health got worse, she became less and less herself. At one time, she would rather have died than impose on someone's time. Her children were the most important things in her life, and she was well down on the list of priorities. Now she was demanding, confused and desperate.

I told friends, "I just wish mom would die! She's miserable, I'm miserable, my family is miserable. If there is some cosmic reason why she's hanging on, I don't see it." Some tried to paint the silver lining for me, saying, "She hung on to see her grandkids. Aren't you glad that they got to know her?" No, I wasn't glad. This wasn't anything like the mother I had known—the great conversationalist, hostess and saucy woman.

The force of my anger permeated all aspects of my life. My husband became a roommate and my children became to-do list items. My friends avoided me. Daily tasks pushed me over the edge. I remember my typical shopping list:

- Bananas
- Clorox wipes
- Carefree maxi pads
- Size 1 Pampers
- Size 6 Pampers
- Small/medium Depends

Why had no one ever noticed the despair that list reflected? Caring for everyone was killing me. I was sure it must be apparent that I was the one in need of care.

I was conflicted all the time. There was no time for me. I stopped working out and put on 20 pounds. It hit me: I had become my mother! Sadly, that wasn't even the lowest point.

Some women from work and I had been looking forward to going to a nationally telecast local golf tournament. I put the kids in daycare for an extra day so I could go. By the time I got to there, the temperature was 90 degrees, and I hadn't eaten since dawn. None of my friends had arrived, but I met others in the same situation. Before I knew it, we had a table of 15 people ordering double screwdrivers. I was a woman again, laughing and flirting, free of all roles. Truly, in that moment, I walked away from all responsibility, and I drank and laughed and drank. By 2 p.m., I had passed out on the seventh hole green in front of two policemen.

I awoke in a hospital. I was ashamed, and yet so sad that it was over. I wanted to stay in the bar, or even in the hospital! I wanted something to be wrong with me so that I could be cared for.

When I got home, my husband couldn't even look at me. I was disgusted with me, too. Perhaps my time for happiness was over. I wanted a mother's lap to crawl into. I wanted her to stroke my hair and tell me I had done enough and was excused from further responsibility.

CHANGING THE STORY

After my meltdown at the golf course, a trusted friend recommended that I call Dr. Andy, who was both a gestalt therapist and practitioner of

Bert Hellinger's approach to family systems.

I'd done the standard therapy thing and thought of myself as rather insightful, so during my first session, I matter of factly stated, "I'm part of the Sandwich Generation."

"The what?"

"The Sandwich Generation—caring for young kids and aging parents." I updated her on my life situation, including the fact that Ryan had taken a job in Connecticut while I remained in Ohio with the kids to sell the house and move my business.

"Anyway," I said, "I don't know why, but I'm mad all the time."

She handed me arrow-shaped sticky notes and instructed me to write the names of family members and place them in order. "The order they are in now, or the order I think they *should* be in?"

"I can't wait until you can stop looking at me for the answers."

Andy observed from my "constellation" that I thought I was stronger than my mother and had to take care of her since day one. "Your story is bullshit," she said. "You are strong, smart, beautiful and athletic. Your parents gave that to you. You must start respecting your mother." I thought therapy was about blaming your parents. What was all this "it's *your* fault" crap?

"But why won't she just go?" I begged Andy to tell me. Then Andy rocked my world. "She isn't hanging on. You are. Until you grow up and care for yourself, she can't leave."

I needed to talk to Mom before she could no longer understand or respond, and I did. I told her that she and Dad were good, strong parents. "There isn't anyone else who would have been a more perfect mother for me."

I asked for her forgiveness for my arrogance, anger and impatience. I told her how devastated I was to see her suffering and that, rather than love her and be so deeply sad, I got mad.

"I know it is hard for you, with your young family," she said. "You do more than I could hope for. You've done more than enough. Thank you."

A few weeks later, Mom went into the hospital with a life-threatening virus in her blood. When I saw her, I knew this was "It." And I could suddenly see all of the karmic reasons why my father sent her back for those last three difficult years.

I held her hand and talked to her quietly. "Mom, I know why Dad sent you back: to save me from living with the anger in my heart forever. He knew that you were strong enough to endure the suffering and that, through it, I would finally see the truth of how much I love you and you love me. If you have to go, know that I am going to take good care of myself. And I am proud of our history."

Four nights later, after around-the-clock shifts, we all went home and slept. A few hours later, the doctor called to tell us mom had just died.

We looked at each other and then out at the sunrise. The pink glow over a frosty hill on a crisp New England morning seemed the perfect escort for a good mother's passing.

NATALIE SHOPE GRIFFIN lives in Andover, Conn. Since her mother's death, she has dedicated herself to family, yoga and shamanic healing. In 2003, she formed Inspire Leadership and continues to help leaders move into their full potential through a unique combination of executive coaching and energetic healing. Her article, "Personalizing Your Leader Development," was published in Harvard Business Review (March 2003) and is featured in the book Harvard Business Review on Developing Leaders. Go to: www.inspireleadership.com

Life, Love, Loss and Rebirth

Never be afraid to risk loving, for it brings the greatest rewards of all

 LORI PHILLIPS GAGNON

As I write this, I am reminded of the famous words, "'Tis better to have loved and lost than never to have loved at all." This saying perfectly sums up the story I am about to tell. For while the ending is tragic, the path was glorious, and this is the part I choose to remember.

THE BEGINNING

On Feb. 7, 2004, I met the man of my dreams. We were at a dinner party, and he was the brother of the hostess. Tom was charming, warm and friendly with a wonderful sense of humor. At 47, he was well traveled, owned a commercial sign company and was creative and artistic. I was 44, self-employed and very happy with my life. Each of us had been divorced for nearly 20 years, and neither of us was looking for love at that moment.

At first sight, I was attracted and felt an instant connection. I feared he might even be too handsome for me!

Tom later told me that it took 15 minutes of begging to get his sister to give him my phone number. But he won out, and the next day he called and asked me to dinner. We clicked, talking and laughing easily. But he was serious, too. He told me he had recently lost his mother to Parkinson's and Alzheimer's. I sensed his sadness, but he was hopeful and positive that the future held wondrous things. At the end of our evening, he asked if he could prepare a Valentine's Day dinner for me. A man who could cook? Of course I said yes.

At the end of May, we visited my family's home in Huntsville, Ala., to surprise my younger sister for her birthday. Tom was an instant hit with my family. They fell in love with his mischievous smile, his spark and his way of making you feel you had known him all your life. And they were thrilled that I had met someone who could help me to trust and to love again.

That weekend, Tom had an urge to ask my father for my hand in marriage. He told Dad that he would only ask me to marry him when he felt he was better able to care for and support me, but he wanted Dad's approval for his plan. Dad was touched by Tom's honesty and devotion to me. He also appreciated Tom's respect for old-fashioned values. Dad couldn't help but give his consent.

Unfortunately, that trip was the only time that Tom would ever have with my father. Dad died unexpectedly five weeks later. Tom accompanied me to Alabama for the funeral, and then I remained there for months, helping my 70-year-old mother learn Dad's end of the direct-mail company they had started in the '80s. Tom was dealing with the end of his own company and starting a new job, so he returned to Florida. But he had experienced the loss of both of his parents, and he was always supportive and reassuring during my period of grief.

Across the miles, we built a wonderful bond as we continued the process of getting to know one another. There were challenges: It was one of the worst summers in Florida for hurricanes, and at times we would be kept from talking for days at a time by downed land lines and overburdened cell phone lines. Yet when we did connect, we shared our fears and dreams. Through long conversations, we discovered how closely aligned our goals and passions were.

By fall of that year, Mom was doing well enough that I was able to leave her for longer periods of time. Tom was feeling more stable in his career, and he planned a getaway for us at the Biltmore Hotel in St. Petersburg. On the last evening we were there, as we sat on the beach watching the sunset, Tom proposed to me.

We were married on March 4, 2005. For the occasion, Tom found the bed-and-breakfast of his dreams in Jackson Hole, Wyo. With our family and friends watching, we exchanged vows before the beautiful fireplace, just as Tom had envisioned. We then went on a sleigh ride over a blanket of fresh snow. The gorgeous backdrop of our wedding was a lovely change of scenery from our home in Florida.

The following month, we purchased our perfect house and moved in and added two kitties, Fritz and Frannie, to our family. Although both of us had been self-employed, we decided that I would enter the nine-to-five workforce for the insurance benefits. Our plans fell into place when I went to volunteer at my church and came home with a job.

Tom had great vision and he loved to create environments of beauty. Whether inside or outside, he tended gardens of plants and flowers, sketched designs for future projects and created gastronomical delights from whatever was available in the refrigerator.

All was well.

THE NEWS

We celebrated our first wedding anniversary filled with joy at having finally found one another. But within the month, Tom's neck inexplicably began to swell. Doctors put him through a battery of tests, and on May 9, 2006, they removed his tonsils, despite the fact that Tom had no pain or typical symptoms. Lab reports revealed Stage 4 cancer in both tonsils, a rare occurrence.

Life as we had known it stopped. Our lives were now filled with doctors and hospitals. Days were dictated by medical tests and the further agony of waiting for results. We suffered disappointment after disappointment.

Tom spent June and July undergoing a new chemotherapy treatment and seven weeks of radiation. There were days and nights he was so sick, unable to eat, swallow or even talk most of the time. He lost 40 pounds and most of his facial hair. By the end of the last treatment, he was even sicker than the doctors had anticipated: He lost 12 pounds in a single week. Still, the prognosis was good. Doctors gave Tom an 85 percent chance of survival.

During the first part of August, Tom started feeling better, and I was able to have a surprise party celebrating his 50th birthday. We were optimistic and held confidently to our faith. We hadn't waited all those years to be together just to be torn apart. At the end of August, his doctors suggested that we take a trip, so we went to Gatlinburg, Tenn., for my niece's wedding. We had a fantastic time, and Tom seemed to be able to eat a bit more and had more energy. All our hope and trust seemed justified.

FIGHT FOR SURVIVAL

But then Tom's progress began to fade. By mid-September, his throat was very painful, and eating was again becoming difficult. His cancer was very aggressive, and tests showed that it had spread, even through the course of chemotherapy and radiation, to the base of his tongue. Tom's chances for survival dropped from 85 percent to 15 percent.

My denial was overwhelming. I focused all my energy on the idea of Tom beating the cancer. I refused to allow myself to think any other way. We listened to every tape and read every book we could find on how to stay positive. We sought alternative healing techniques, all the while praying for a miracle. Tom rejected any negativity. He would say only that he wanted to live and everything would be fine.

We were referred to M.D. Anderson Cancer Institute in Orlando, and then sent to Houston for further evaluation. But doctors said there was nothing more they could do for him. He was given a prognosis of four to six months to live. We were sent back to Orlando for additional chemotherapy to alleviate symptoms and control the spread of the disease. He responded well to the first few rounds, and our hopes again burned brightly. Tom's optimism somehow helped me push through fears and doubt.

The day after our second wedding anniversary, we received news that the chemotherapy in fact was not working. Tom's aggressive cancer had wrapped around the carotid arteries in his neck. We now had another decision to make. We agreed that we wanted to spend our remaining time together without Tom being so sick that he could barely think straight. With feelings of fear and shock alternating with numbness, I witnessed the disappointment and sadness on Tom's face as he lovingly thanked the doctors for all they had done and told them he would not seek additional treatment. He elected to continue with hospice at home, although he still clung to hope that his situation would somehow improve.

FINAL ACCEPTANCE

The hospice caregivers were wonderful. The last month of Tom's life we had almost around-the-clock care. Tom loved his nurses and would insist that we pray for each one at the change of shifts. Their presence helped me to get the rest I needed, so I could stay focused on making the best choices for Tom and keep him surrounded by love and comfort. At times I would silently cry, as the thought of losing him slowly began to sink into my heart and mind. The wonderful man I married seemed to be disappearing before my very eyes. I tried not to let the change in his appearance, behavior and ability affect me, but it took a toll. My strength and encouragement came from the love and support of my family, our church family and especially Tom's sister, Mary Joe, who was with us daily.

Tom wanted me to read to him or just sit and "take it nice and smooth"—his words, which he would write to me when he could no longer talk. His child-like faith and actions were endearing to every one who spent time with him. I was his number one fan.

I struggled to hide my fear and pain, especially from Tom. I was so angry that he was sick, and so sad for all the unfulfilled dreams and goals that we would not accomplish together. Never had I been more alone and anxious about the future. I also experienced deep feelings that I was being disloyal to Tom, as he held such a fierce belief that he would be healed and I felt him slipping away. I was afraid that I wouldn't survive losing him.

After stopping medical treatment, we continued to try anything and everything possible—acupuncture, "miracle" drinks, vitamins—to halt the disease in its tracts. But it wasn't meant to be.

On April 5, 2007, surrounded by family, Tom slipped away from this earth even as I held him in my arms.

MOVING THROUGH THAT FIRST YEAR

At first I counted the days that he was gone, then the weeks, then the months. Now it has been a year. How I still long to hear his voice, see his smile, feel his hand hold mine or just listen to the sound of his breathing as he lays beside me in bed. The reality of my loss slowly creeps in with each new day. There are still bouts of tears when I need to share something with him and realize I can't.

The first few months I craved meeting others who had been through the loss of a spouse to know if what I was feeling was "normal." Is it normal to feel OK one minute and the next minute feel such overwhelming sorrow and dread that you just want to hide under the bed?

Inconsolable grief would sweep over me and take my breath away with each cruel decision and step I had to take: sorting through his clothes, his desk, his email; discovering anew the notes and cards he gave me, the pictures he drew for me; hearing his voicemail message on the answering machine. I thought the deep sorrow would never leave me or let me rest, yet a year later there are more good days than sad ones. The guilt of living has dissipated and does not rule my life.

I go through the motions every day, hoping to get a little wiser, a little stronger and more compassionate toward others living with the pain and grief of losing a loved one. I started healing through a Hospice Widows support group. I do cranio-sacral bodywork, a holistic therapy that relieves pain and alleviates other ailments, including mental stress. I allow myself to be honest about how I feel. I cry when I feel like crying. I haven't tried to be brave and hide my emotions, and I do feel that helped me release much of the anger and pain.

The difficult decisions—taking off my wedding rings, selling his truck, dealing with all his tools—happened when it was time. At six months, I moved my engagement ring to my right hand and tucked my wedding band into a keepsake box with his.

I often wished there was a guide, one book with all the "correct" answers on how to do everything that needs to be done when your spouse has died. Yet, through this trial, I have learned that we all have our own path, our own lessons to learn, and our own way to deal with the struggles of life. No one's route is the same as the next person's. It is about how we get there, how we learn to love others and allow others to love us through the good and bad times.

Occasionally I feel like I am betraying Tom by continuing to live my life. At those times I focus on one thought: "What would I want Tom to be doing if it had been me who died?" Knowing that guilt is not what I would want him to feel, I push on. I want to use the memory of Tom as an encouragement to live my life as fully as I possibly can, not something to hold myself back from taking a risk in life.

From time to time I struggle with loneliness and a fear of what will happen next, but I have not lost faith that there is a purpose for my life. I have not closed myself off from the world, as I so wanted to do right after Tom died. By continuing to go through the motions of what a normal life should have been for me this last year, I am beginning to emerge from the pain and sorrow and feel the strength and joy of living life as Tom would want me to.

During this first year, I didn't make any major job or life changes.

And, as I look back on the year without Tom, here is what gave me comfort and strength to move forward:

- Daily phone calls with my mother,
- Joining a hospice support group,
- Being able to be honest about my feelings to my friends and family,
- Support of my church, and
- Taking really good care of myself (sleeping or crying when I needed to).

Tom will never be far from my thoughts as his spirit is planted deep in my heart. I will always carry the passion that Tom had for family, friends and nature. He was a very happy, positive fellow!

Although our time together on this earth may have been short, we lived an entire lifetime in those three years and two months together.

May any of you going through a similar situation, who have recently lost a loved one, remember that adage I quoted at the beginning: "'Tis better to have loved and lost, than never to have loved at all."

For me, the beauty of the journey was absolutely worth the pain.

Born in Bryan, Ohio, **LORI PHILLIPS GAGNON** lives in Orlando, Fla., where she met and married Tom. Prior to that, she lived and worked in central Europe, setting up call centers for a large telecommunications company. After returning to the United States, she took cooking classes at a local health food store and met Bill Hettig. Together they created The Perfect Pickler™, the revolutionary pickling device featured on HGTV. For details, visit www.PerfectPickler.com or call (877) 505-9053.

The Bottom Line: Balancing Family and Career

How one woman maintains the hectic pace of home and business

 DEBRA TAYLOR

As I approach the 10th anniversary of the founding of my wealth management firm, Taylor Financial Group, I see that the "Road to 10" has been filled with challenges and opportunities that have helped to define me as a person.

I did not just stumble upon wealth management as a profession, but neither was it my lifelong goal to manage money. My childhood dream was to become an attorney, which I am. I graduated near the top of my class from an Ivy League law school and landed a prestigious clerkship with the chief judge of the federal district court of my home state, New Jersey. I next accepted a job as an associate at a very large law firm. Both jobs enabled me to work with great attorneys who were leaders in their field and men and women of virtue. But after working for several years in these roles, I was persuaded by my mother to join the family tax and accounting practice that my father had started in the 1950s. On her insistence, I returned to school in accounting at the age of 26 and passed the CPA exam. At 28, I assumed leadership of the family business and happily continued my frenetic work pace.

The tax practice was busy, as we prepared more than 1,000 returns each tax season, and we developed many meaningful relationships over the years. While working as a tax professional, I identified a need among our clients for principled advice on their finances in general. Many clients who approached me had no idea about their investments, and some had never even met their financial advisers. These people were investing blindly with their stockbrokers, but had no plan or vision for the future. Would they be able to retire at age 63, as they desired? Would they be able to pay for their children to attend college, as they had dreamed? They had no idea if any of their aspirations would come true, as no one was working with them to identify goals, much less to see to it that those goals were achieved. Instead, at best, the focus was on the hot stock tip of the day; mostly, there was no communication at all with their so-called "financial advisers." By the time a client would realize what had happened, it would be too late. Achieving life goals requires years of planning and deliberation and hard work with a financial adviser.

DEFEATING FEAR AND INSECURITY

I felt compassion for these people who had been so ill-served by the traditional relationships with stockbrokers/advisers. So, in addition to working at the tax practice, I decided to start a financial planning business, because, plain and simple, I had a desire to provide security for myself and others. As a child, I understood the fear and insecurity that accompanies an uncertain financial future. When I was 10 years old, my father died unexpectedly of a heart attack. Overnight, my life changed forever. On that day, my mother became the sole breadwinner and only parent to three children.

Over time, my mother grew the tax and accounting practice and began buying commercial real estate. She became a successful and admired businesswoman, well known in the community. But the fear, uncertainty and sense of loss that we endured during those years are things that I vowed never to allow to repeat in my own life. And my childhood experience enabled me to provide compassionate advice to my clients, particularly in their times of distress.

Although I have all types of clients—husbands and wives, families, individuals, institutions and same sex couples—my favorite clients are women, as I feel we are able to accomplish great things together. Some of my women clients are recently widowed, lost in a sea of paperwork,

emotions, confusion and bureaucracy. Often, they have never managed their own affairs, and may not know what the real estate taxes on their homes are or even how to balance a checkbook. I educate and empower them. We discuss not only finances, but also their goals for themselves and their families and their fears—fears of running out of money or of spending their entire estate on healthcare needs. These relationships are most gratifying as I have the privilege of participating in the growth of an individual from a dependent wife to a self-assured independent woman.

I also enjoy my work with newly divorced women, for much the same reasons. Although the circumstances differ, the process is similar as we help these women to become independent and in charge of their lives. The challenges are greater for divorced women who have young children at home, which complicates their ability to work and provides additional expenses. However, many of these women adapt amazingly well, searching deep to determine their passions or hidden talents and then converting those talents into a living, all while raising their children and managing their homes. I say bravo to these women as their roads are not easy, and I am happy to support them in their new roles.

I also work with women still in a marriage. I listen to their concerns and integrate their philosophies and needs into our decisions. Sometimes, married women are not confident enough in expressing their views and encourage hiring my firm as a way to gain a voice in the management of the family finances. I work to empower them in their relationships.

REACHING A CROSSROADS

As a woman, I relate to the special demands on women. And my own financial life has had its challenges. At around the same time that I was running the family practice and trying to build my own business, I got married and immediately became pregnant with our first child, Caroline. Although our hours were long, my husband and I managed to maintain the busy work schedule and devote all of our free time to Caroline. Then, within two years, I became pregnant with our second child, Cecilia, and felt that I had reached a crossroads. Indeed, within two weeks of Cece's birth, I experienced an epiphany. I knew that I could not maintain the pace of running two businesses *and* raising children without something "giving in"—either my health and well-being, my children's health and well-being, or my clients' welfare. None of these compromises was acceptable to me. Thus, over the strenuous objections of my mother, I decided to sell the tax and accounting practice and focus exclusively on the wealth management firm. Within a month, the deed was done. I had sold the family business, which had been in existence for more than 40 years.

The transition was difficult. My family was unsupportive, to say the least. And while I had developed clients for the wealth management firm, the tax practice had been the much better established business and had provided a much steadier source of income. In addition, I was soon to have a third child. Most important to me was to be available to my children. Many of the decisions that were put in place allowed me to do that. I still try to be home every day when they arrive from school, and I attend their soccer games and school activities. Although this balancing act makes for a hectic life—I work almost every night after the children go to sleep—I know that I've done what I can to balance my life and to stay true to my purpose.

PURSUING A VISION

Still, I had a vision for the business I wanted to build and the type of service I wanted to provide. I created a "fee-based" practice so that my interests could be aligned with my clients. Although today, in most instances, a fee-based model is considered best practices, it was certainly a minority viewpoint when I was starting out. In the traditional pricing structure, the stockbroker charges a large up-front commission (that the client may or may not know about), and then often has no incentive to further service the account unless he or she believes that more assets can be gathered from the client or more commissions created. In stark contrast to this pricing scheme, the fee-based method incentivized me to continue serving my clients at an extraordinary level throughout an entire relationship.

While, at times, I have had to turn down business to maintain the balance in my life, some of my peers accept anyone who walks through the door. As a result, their books have grown much faster than my own, and they sometimes bring home higher incomes. However, they enter into contracts in which their intentions are faulty. They make commitments, however subtle, that they will continue caring for and servicing these clients when, in fact, they do not have the ability to uphold their end of the contracts. I never felt comfortable in approaching my business relationships in this way. When you become a client of our firm, you enter into a "family." I treat my older clients the way I would treat my mother or father and my younger clients the way I would treat a niece or nephew. This level of compassion and connectedness has earned us the lasting loyalty of our clients.

Throughout the year, we try to find ways to acknowledge those we serve. We call them on their birthdays and send them birthday cakes (baked by a nonprofit foundation that assists substance-dependent women in rebuilding their lives). And every Thanksgiving, we send a book or some other "gratitude" gift to remind all our clients how much we care about them and to gently remind them that we should all be grateful. For example, last year we sent the book, *The Ultimate Gift*, by Jim Stovall and Dawn Billings, about a fictional billionaire and the lessons he imparts to his nephew about the meaning of "success." We received such a positive response from the mailing of this book that we are sending *The Ultimate Gift* video this Thanksgiving. These gifts and our firm's other outreach activities, in addition to our service model, are what set us apart from other money managers.

Maintaining my vision for the business provided the only hope on some days. Remaining steadfast in the execution of that vision, day by day and year by year, required commitment and enormous discipline. Over the years, with our ups and downs, it has worked. We have created a well-respected wealth management firm that was ranked in the Top 15 of all firms at our previous broker-dealer for two years in a row. I was the first woman to ever attain that honor. Our firm continues to be ranked as a "top producer," despite (or because of) our client service model. I have focused on the sustainable growth of my business, creating success on my own terms.

Being a financial planner allows me to help people I care

about. As a woman, it is in my nature to care about people and to build connections. Through my work as a financial planner, I am fortunate to make a difference in so many lives, in a way that feels meaningful to me.

DEBRA TAYLOR, CPA/PPS, Esq., investment advisory representative, is the principal of Taylor Financial Group, LLC, a full-service wealth management firm in Franklin Lakes, N.J. Because of her education and experience, she is able to provide a multidisciplinary approach to meet her clients' needs. Debra lives in Franklin Lakes with her husband and three children. She enjoys time with her family, aerobics, tennis, travel and reading. Visit her website at www.Taylorfinancialgroup.com and sign up for her Weekly Market Commentary.

Forging Strength Through Adversity

Unlocking the healing powers of the mind and heart

SUSAN GLAVIN

This story is for anyone who has lost a loved one, is losing a loved one or even those who are fortunate enough to still have their loved ones with them, especially their parents.

It begins at Portland International Airport in June of 2006. I had just stepped off of the plane, and as I made my way to the baggage claim, I saw my husband walking toward me. This was unusual, as I would typically call him on my cell phone after my bags arrived, and he would pick me up outside. Was something wrong? He quietly told me that my mother had seen a doctor who believed she had cancer.

Time stopped. A wave of emotion filled my body. I can't even tell you what the emotion was, as I've never felt it before or since. I wanted to scream and cry, but, surrounded by people waiting for their bags, I held it back.

On the way to my mother's house, questions rattled around in my head. The most powerful one was, "What do we do now?"

THE FIRST DECISION

I have always believed that the best medicine is a natural one; most people would call this "alternative medicine." I think that statement gets the sequence backward. It was *natural* medicine that we began with, and it is *alternative* medicine that most medical doctors practice today.

While I am aware of many resources for natural healing, not only on the physical level but also the emotional and spiritual ones, I know a patient must decide for herself what she *believes* will be the best course of action—"alternative" or "traditional" treatment. Belief is key. Mother chose both—a combination of natural medicine and chemotherapy.

Mother's first appointment was with an oncologist. All four of her daughters were there to support her and hear the plan the doctor had for eradicating the cancer. The doctor walked into the room with a bit of a surprise on his face, as he was greeted by five very anxious women. After introductions, he immediately started rattling off statistics. I remember wanting to say, "Stop! We don't want to hear or believe what you are saying."

"Your mother has small cell carcinoma," he told us. "The CAT scan shows it in her lungs and the lymph nodes in her neck. There is a 1 to 2 percent chance of survival. The type of chemotherapy we have to use to fight the cancer is very hard on the kidneys. It sometimes gets to the point of kidney failure, which would result in her having to start dialysis. This type of cancer is very aggressive and can metastasize to the bones and ultimately to the brain, where we would then have to start radiating her brain."

It was like he was handing out facts at a business meeting. The staggering statistics went on and on, but I can't remember much more of what the doctor said. I had recently become aware of how what we believe affects the results that we create or manifest in our lives, and I was concerned about my mother hearing this. As I looked at her face, I wanted to grab her and run out of the room. I wanted to save her from listening to and believing everything that the doctor was saying.

Even with my awareness about the power of thoughts, I found myself believing this doctor knew what was best for my mother. After all, he was the expert, the one with all the degrees. I, too, wanted to look to others to tell us what we should do, instead of looking to ourselves for the answers. How easily we give up our power and inner knowing to someone we think knows more then we do about our lives!

THE NATURAL APPROACH

I can't tell you how grateful I was when later that same day we all met with a naturopathic doctor who had been highly recommended by my sister's midwife. This was quite a different experience. After a two-hour consultation and exam, we left with a plan of action that included herbal remedies to support her vital organs and weekly hydrotherapy treatments of hot and cold wraps to support her immune system. More important, the doctor reminded us that it was up to my mother as to what she believed was best for her. He gently handed her power back to her. It was up to her to take it. Her relief was palpable in getting a plan that offered the possibility of healing and life.

My sisters and I looked for more ways to support our mother during this challenging time in all of our lives. A dear family friend who is a therapist, healer and minister offered heartfelt, compassionate conversation along with the services of a Rife machine, healing frequencies and the NRG machine, which is used to do detoxifying foot baths.

So it began for my mother. The weekly trips to chemotherapy, hydrotherapy, sessions on the Rife machine, daily herbs, tonics and vitamins to support her body while they pumped in the poison that she hoped would save her.

Her naturopath explained to us that the purpose of the hydrotherapy was to create what is called a "healing crisis." During this time, my mother could become very sick, but it would be vital that she allow her body to heal on its own, without medication of any kind, during the crisis. This would then make her immune system much stronger, enabling her body to ward off the cancer. I see this "healing crisis" as a powerful metaphor for life. Aren't the most difficult and challenging times in our life when we gain the most strength, wisdom and healing?

MORE ABOUT THE WOMAN

Before I continue the story of her battle, I would like to tell you a little bit about Nadean Pedro, our mother. As a young woman, one of her dreams was to become a nurse. But that was but on the back burner as she became pregnant after dating our father a couple of months. Five children later—four girls and a boy—that dream completely faded away.

We grew up in what most people would label a highly dysfunctional home. Looking back, I can see the tremendous courage our mother had and the sacrifices she made to keep our family together. She made every attempt to keep the peace in a home whose foundation was built on anger, fear and uncertainty.

Through this, she never missed a day's work, and to my knowledge, the only commitment she didn't keep was when she divorced our father after 39 years of marriage. The divorce gave him the opportunity to discover just how angry a man he was. He then started to live his life from a much more loving place.

Volunteer work was important to my mother. She volunteered at the county courthouse for 18 years. She still holds the church record for the number of years she volunteered as the hospitality hostess.

My mother didn't always express how she was feeling. She held many things inside. I think the phrase for this is "close to the chest." I understand why she felt she had to keep it all inside. There was no alternative with five wounded, angry children and one pissed-off husband. If she had expressed her feelings, she may have just walked out the door and never looked back. Like many mothers, she tried to keep the boat from rocking or, better yet, capsizing. But I now wonder if her inability to express emotion was a leading cause of her illness. All that anger, pain, fear and sadness lived inside her. Was the cancer their way of showing their ugly faces?

CRISIS TO HEALING TO CRISIS

Mother's strength and courage were evident as she went through the difficult stages of chemotherapy. Rarely did I hear her complain during the hair loss, fatigue, nausea and endless appointments.

Then it happened…the healing crisis we had been waiting for. Thankfully, my sister was living with her at the time and was able to care for her. Mother became so sick that it was difficult for me to trust that this was part of the healing process. At one point, we had to call the naturopath to come to her home and examine her as she was too weak to make it to his office.

Days passed and finally she seemed to be getting stronger and feeling like her old self. She even felt good enough to pig out on ice cream.

I was so grateful to be able to go with her to oncology appointment one day in February 2007. We were hoping for good results from the CAT scan. Well, the results were not good—they were great! There were no signs of cancer! The oncologist couldn't explain to us why this had happened.

This was a day to celebrate, we couldn't wait to get on the phone and start calling our family and friends to tell them the great news.

Then there was a series of events the following day, Feb. 24, 2007.

Thinking she was stable and sleeping comfortably, I ran some errands with my husband. But we soon got the dreaded call. My sister, distressed and panicky said, "She stopped breathing!"

"Call 911!" I screamed

"I already did."

We were only five minutes away, but still another call came before we could reach the house. "Where are Mom's will and her directive for resuscitation?" my sister asked.

"What? Why? What is happening?" I cried. "Oh my God."

"She stopped breathing for quite a while," she said. "They want her directives."

"I don't know. Hang on. I'm almost there."

Again, I was at a place I had never experienced. My mind and body were hardly able to contain what was happening inside. The emotion was all consuming and *more*.

As we turned the corner, I could see the fire truck and ambulance. I leaped from the car and ran toward the house.

FIGHTING FOR MOTHER

As I ran down the hall to my mother's room, I saw my sister in one of the rooms crying, trying to find the directives. As I made my way to the open door of my mother's room, I saw several paramedics working to revive her. Her still, naked body lay on the floor next to her bed. I fell to my knees and began to plead with God.

Out of the room came a loud shout. The tall fire chief demanded mother's life directives or he said he would instruct the paramedics to stop resuscitation.

I got as close to his red face as I could and screamed back, "Back off, buddy. That is my mother in there!"

My sister chimed in, "She just beat cancer, and you do whatever you can!" Talk about not giving our power away. We knew what was best for us.

I walked to the kitchen, furious. With tears streaming down my face, I screamed from the depth of my soul, "NOT TODAY!" Seconds later the very apologetic fire chief came into the kitchen to say, "We have a pulse."

"Thank you, God! Thank you, God!" were the words that came to me as we ran to our cars to follow the ambulance to the hospital.

Calls were made to family and friends. My brother was driving a long haul truck and my sister was on vacation in California. I'm certain it was a long and painful journey back home for both of them.

One of the most difficult calls to make was to my 81-year-old father. After all the years of pain and struggle in their relationship, my parents had become dear friends, and I know they still loved each other deeply.

I believe that my mother knew her family wasn't ready to let her go. She knew that we needed more time to get our minds and hearts around the idea that it was her time to go. So she stayed a few more days, for us.

FINDING PEACE AND COMFORT

It was still difficult for some of us to let her go. We just wanted a little more time, to hug her, to tell her how much she meant in our lives, to see her smile one more time. So she made that decision for us. The morning of Feb. 27, 2007, we received a call telling us it was only a matter of time.

At the hospital, we gathered around her as her spirit left her body and filled the room with stillness and peace. I will always remember that moment.

The events and miracles that happened in the hours and days that followed with the presence and love of our mother are many. A cherished moment was just after my sisters and I left the hospital and went to mother's home. We were standing in the kitchen crying and laughing, telling old stories, when we noticed Mother's angel cards on the dining room table. My mother loved her angel cards and would pick from the deck to receive messages from the angels she knew were with her. My sister remembered when Mother drew her last angel card. How happy she had been with the message—"Triumphant"—with a picture of the guardian angel on the front of the card. So we all decided to draw a card. We said a prayer and laid them out on the table. My sister picked one. TRIUMPHANT! We screamed, cried out and held each other, knowing that our mother was sending us this message. What a powerful and blessed moment! To this day, Mother visits me in my dreams and gives me many signs that she is always with us.

Looking back, I am so grateful for the times that I sat with my mother at her kitchen table. Times when I told her not only that I loved her, but what it was that I loved about her—her intelligence, her dedication, how she was always willing to give and serve in any way that she could. I thanked her for showing me great work ethic and discipline.

I forgave her for not leaving our father when we were young. It wasn't until I started working with women who had experienced domestic violence that I understood why Mother felt she had to stay with him. I told her I wasn't angry anymore. It was her weakness that has given me tremendous strength today. Her eyes filled with tears, and as hard as it was for her to receive my words, I know she did take in what I shared with her.

LEARNING FROM LIFE

It took my realizing how living in the past was paralyzing my life today to help me find that strength. All I had to do was to be willing, willing to stop blaming, judging and being a victim of the past. To start looking at what was right about it, instead of what was wrong. What were the gifts, the lessons and wisdom that my mother so willingly gave to me?

The family's experience with our mother's illness and death made me realize not only the importance of letting those we love know how we feel about them, but also the importance of family in our lives. Each one of her children brought a special piece to our mother's life during her difficult time.

What I want to leave you with is this: If you fortunate enough to have one or both of your parents with you, take the time to discover what it is that they have contributed to you life. What do you love and appreciate about them? What is it that you need to forgive them for? Forgiveness is one of the biggest gifts you can give to them and, more important, to yourself. When they are gone, it will be those moments that will give you great peace in a time of deep sorrow.

My mother had beaten her cancer. I remember her oncologist was speechless the day we got the results that there were no traces of cancer in her body. She had turned what looked like a death sentence into an opportunity. She learned how to express how she was feeling, to be vulnerable and ask for help. She opened her heart to the possibility that there was more to life then what she had been lead to believe.

My mother believed she could heal from cancer, and she did. It was the chemotherapy that caused her to have a heart attack, resulting in her death.

What we believe to be true, the emotions we have about those beliefs greatly affect our physical and emotional selves. Be diligent about your thoughts and beliefs; they do impact your life. Make the journey from "victim" to "victor."

I've learned that you always know what is the best decision or choice for yourself. Notice when you give up your power to an outside authority instead of looking to your inner authority. Trust in the power in *you*!

Be willing to let go of the past, to forgive yourself and others for mistakes made. Learn from them, grow from them and expand from them into who you really are.

This is really my mother's message. It came to me through a mother's love, for her family and the people's lives it may touch, move or inspire.

I want to thank my amazing, weak, gracious, scared and courageous mother for giving me this experience and wisdom. Through her process of dying, I am able to embrace all of who I am, which in turn I give to you.

SUSAN GLAVIN, founder of Moving the World Forward, developed her powerful seminars to teach and inspire people to discover their passions and live their purpose. She is a Master Clarity Coach, passion test facilitator, certified PSYCH-K™ practitioner, trained in the Law of Attraction. Visit her website at www.MovingTheWorldForward.com and signup for her monthly e-zine, "Your Passion in Action."

Make Room in the Boys' Club!

True leadership, not competition, paves the way

 ROBIN HUGHES

Talk about being a woman in a man's world! That's me. As a child, I was a tomboy and spent my summers playing in orange groves in Florida, being every boy's "best bud." Softball, swimming, volleyball, soccer—you name the sport, I played it. As a teenager, I spent summers on a ski boat with all my best buds; in my off-season, I was the equipment manager for the boys' baseball team.

In college, I diversified. I'll never forget the day I called my dad and told him, "My psychology class was so interesting! I'd love to have a career in this field. I think I'm gonna declare psychology as my major." There was an uncomfortably long silence on the line before he said, "Why don't you take a business class?" Dad was right. I went on to major in business and accounting.

The three best pieces of advice I ever got from my dad were:

1. Don't gamble the rent money. (Who can argue with that classic piece of fatherly wisdom?)
2. Tell the truth and then you don't have to remember what you said. (Another classic!)
3. And … take a business class.

Despite my new interests, nothing dimmed my passion for sports and hanging with my best buds. Soon after I arrived at Wake Forest University, I saw a flyer on the bulletin board seeking equipment managers for the football team. I walked down to the field in the middle of practice, asked about the position and was directed to the head equipment manager.

Picture a former-drill sergeant barking out commands, standing on one leg while holding the other one—a prosthesis—in his hand. (He lost his leg during his second tour of duty in Vietnam.) I told him I had experience as an equipment manager and wanted the job. He choked out a laugh and replied, "Girls don't do that job." "They didn't yesterday," I replied. An assistant coach nearby started laughing, but Sarge (yes, he really was called that) was impressed and hired me with a terse, "Be at the equipment room at 1 p.m. tomorrow." (As if I knew where that was? I sure as heck wasn't going to ask!) He told me later that he thought I would be crying and running for my life that first day.

BLAZING A TRAIL

But I succeeded against the odds. And after three years of withstanding coaches' brow-beatings, enduring ice storm practices, loading planes on runways and traveling by U-Haul all over the country, I became the first female NCAA Division I senior equipment manager for football. Whenever I'd walk into an opposing team's locker room, heads would turn. I literally "heard" silence, as people stopped what they were doing to stare.

A woman in a man's world? You bet. And it didn't stop there.

When I got out of college with my shiny new accounting degree, I went to work for a sports marketing company. We promoted NASCAR and PGA tour events, which involved tons of travel and, of course, hanging with the boys.

When I moved back to Tampa, I applied for an accounting job at the headquarters of the Tampa Bay Lightning hockey team. I met with the CFO, and he didn't hire me. "The nerve," I thought. "He must be insane." So I went to work at a huge financial services company instead. After two months of wanting to stick a pin in my eye every day, I called up the Lightning's CFO and asked how the new hire was working out. After a slight hesitation, he said, "He gave his notice today." "Would you like to meet with me again?" I asked. With no hesitation this time, he asked, "Can you get here by 6:00 tonight?" The rest is history.

The Tampa Bay Lightning was sold twice while I was there. I rose through the ranks to become the controller of the team, but then I started to lose interest in accounting. I became sick of just reporting on the finances; I wanted to be part of the action. I didn't want to just show the box office manager a report that demonstrated how a sales rep had stolen $14,000. I wanted to be that guy's boss and get to look him in the eye as I told him he was fired. I wanted to create efficiencies for companies that actually made money. I wanted to set policies in place that made a company *go*, not just look at the action through the rearview mirror. It was time to move on.

I went to work for a software development and consulting company. It took about a year for me to take over the training and technical support departments, even while I was continuing to do accounting and preparing the consulting division for a spin-off. In the meantime, I met an amazing woman in a mastermind group who talked about her business with excitement and joy. When Kathy and I worked on business issues in the group, she had a way of looking at problems from a human instead of a technical perspective. I had been in the group about a year when I began commenting on my frustration at not have enough decision-making authority. "You are like us," Kathy said, referring to her firm. "Tell me when you're ready and come work with us." I was honored and freaked out at the same time, but ever decisive.

I went to the president/owner of the software company and said, "I'm ready. I need to run something." He looked at me curiously and said, "But that's my job, and it's all I know how to do." It was time to part ways. Luckily, Kathy was waiting for me, and I went for an interview.

During our negotiation on compensation, Kathy asked me how much I needed to make. I gave her a number, and she said, "I have no idea if I can afford you. Will you look at my books to see?" Did I mention she has a radically different business approach that involves honesty and openness? I looked at the books and said, "You can't *not* afford me. I'll get the money from right here... and here... and here." I pointed to line items that I could change so the company would actually save money by hiring me.

I began to pick up speed in my learning, and I started to believe in myself and my ability to conquer any challenge, even an organization full of auto mechanics. That's right! Kathy ran an auto repair franchising company. That's what I had left my corporate job for.

It was important to me to run a business I could be proud of, and just making money was not an acceptable scorecard. I served notice to almost 40 percent of the company's 21 franchisees that they either start acting right or it would be "adios!" Several weren't interested in changing, so we parted ways. One tried to fight, and it took me six weeks to get him forcibly evicted. Those were trying times, and it was a big shift for me to stay rigorously sure of the mission. I faced criticism from franchisees, my employees and even my partners. I was scared, and frankly I'm still scared. I lie awake nights not sure if it's all going to work out. But I know that no matter the end result, it *is* going to work out because I'm following what I believe in.

UNLOCKING THE SECRET

I'm often asked how to break into a man's world of business. I used to think it was acting like a man that did it, and I got pretty far with that belief. Now I have a new understanding that I would love to pass on so other women don't have to learn the hard way, as I did. I used to concentrate on competing—compete, win; compete, win; keep score; get ahead. But none of this really tied into what I wanted in my heart. There was a shift from being an employee to being a manager to being a leader.

I study leadership, and I've narrowed my view of it down to one principle: *Be worthy of people following you.* That's what true leadership is. No title I ever had made me a leader. When I stop playing roles and am just myself, that self is somebody pretty cool. That woman wants other people to have success, and she wants to leave behind something good in the world. Other people are attracted to her. True leadership is in self-improvement.

Here's how I do it every day:

- **Slow down to speed up.** For a long time, that sounded like such stupid advice that I never gave it any credence. Now it's my motto. I can fill my life up with busy, busy, busy, but since I've made a conscious effort to slow down, I can achieve more. I've decided that "busy" is a lie, an illusion to enable avoidance. My least productive days are the ones where there's something to be done that I don't want to do, so I avoid it by staying busy with everything else. I stay busy to lie to myself that I can't get to the thing I should have done.

- **Build relationships.** The most important work I do is on the relationships I build. And here's the great news for many women: we're naturals at this! Frankly, we have an unfair advantage in a man's world. My resume speaks for itself that I can get "stuff" done. The time I spend on people sends ripple effects into the world unlike any task that I could check off my to-do list. I am drawn to helping people, and it's a beautiful feminine quality.

- **Self-care and balance count.** I've become increasingly more effective as a leader as my self-care has improved. Quality self-care started by being more honest with myself. I had a gym membership for ages and never went. I finally realized that I wasn't ever going to go, so I hired a trainer. I knew that if someone was there tapping her foot waiting for me to show up, I would. I adapted to what I would do, then took it up another notch. I've lost 30 pounds.

- **Stop proving you're worthwhile to everyone else.** A big part of my "achieving in a man's world" was just proving that I could do it. My life got a lot better when I stopped trying to please everyone else. I believe that the people in my life saw I was happier because I was able to be more direct and consistent. It was easier to make the changes in my work life as I was already used to being in charge. This is still a big work in progress in my personal life. It was hard at first because I had spent so many years ignoring my beautiful, wise, quiet, genuine voice that I couldn't hear it anymore. In the simplest situations where I was being asked about a personal preference, I was stumped. I would literally have to stop and think, "Do I want Mexican or Chinese?"

A wise female mentor of mine says, "Being genuine is the only thing that really matters." There's an invincibility I didn't expect that comes from being genuine. No one can see through me, burst my bubble or tell me I don't know what I'm talking about. I totally own it! I can control my own genuineness completely. I can say, "I don't know what that word means," or "I'm not familiar with that. Tell me about it." I used to work so hard at proving my worth to everyone else that I lived in fear of people finding me out, finding out that I don't know what I'm talking about, or that I'm not smart enough or whatever my insecurity *du jour* was.

- **Live your life!** And live deeply! Not being plugged into the TV or going to your 9-to-5 existence, but living in *real life*. Crying, laughing and accomplishing. Life was not meant to be easy, so live deeply! I *always* did more than the minimum. It's an honor to be nominated ... ha! Show me second place and I'll show you the first loser. Anything worth having is worth fighting for.

- **Ask for help!** Boy, could I muscle through any situation like a champ. Asking for help was the ultimate weakness in my book. If other people knew that I didn't know something, I thought, they would exploit that advantage and take something away from me that I should have. When I started asking for help, life got better.

When I stopped doing everything for my staff (because if you want something done right, you have to do it yourself ... not!) life got better for all of us. My team loves it because I am more consistent and clear. They used to run around not sure whether I was doing a project or they were, then I would get mad when stuff had to be finished at the last minute. (Have I mentioned that I've turned over a lot of staff to get here? Who could work for me as I used to be?)

I've even taken asking for help to a new level: I ask other *women* for help. I really started waking up to my own abilities after another woman gave me an opportunity to be myself. She recognized how worthy I am, and I was able to start believing it.

- **Be gentle with yourself.** You are a work in progress, and no one is harder on you than yourself. Pay attention to the tapes you play in your mind, and if you don't like the message, change the tape! It's an adventure for me because I still have all the old tapes mixed in with my new ones. So, when someone compliments me, my old tape says, "She's just being nice. If she only knew how dumb you are...." I have to consciously stop that tape and say, "She thinks I am smart. Thank her for noticing and be grateful to her for noticing this wonderful truth about me." Here's another example: The old tape says: "Keep her at arm's length. That's how you protect yourself, how you stay in control. She'll just hurt you with the information anyway." The new tape says: "Tell her that you are scared that you are going to screw this up. Tell her the story about how you did screw something up and let her help you."

- **Yes, you can have it all.** Another mantra I had as I was scratching and clawing through a man's world was: No one has it all. I'd think, "Those pretty girls (that I was jealous of) could *not* be as smart as me." Or, "That girl is smart, but I'll bet her family is so screwed up, and her husband probably cheats on her." On and on I'd go with this negative dialogue. I could have found a cure for world hunger by now if I had managed to harness all my wasted mental energy and put it toward something other than my massive, steaming pile of insecurities. I used to take myself so seriously and felt I had to be the smartest person in the room. I had to know more facts than anyone else and achieve more. Laugh at myself? Certainly not!

How do I accept these total flake parts of myself and be kind to myself at the same time? I've learned to let go. I now rejoice in the weird moments of confusion when I can't order off a menu or someone asks, "Do you like going to New York on vacation?" and I don't have a ready answer. I've run big companies for years without having any clue whether I like linguine or angel hair pasta better. Just imagine how amazing I'll be at it when I can make big decisions like that!

- **Live in gratitude.** I am grateful for all the experiences that have made up my journey on this road of life. I am more alive everyday because of each one of them. I am also grateful for my lover, my partners, my friends, my family and everyone who touches my life ... strike that, everyone I allow to touch my life.

Can a woman succeed in a man's world? She sure can ... as long as she's a success in her own world first!

ROBIN HUGHES lives in Tampa, Fla. In a career dominated by "man's world" jobs, including controller of the Tampa Bay Lightning and vice president of Ideal Software, she is president of franchisor Ice Cold Air Discount Auto Repair. She's compiled a free report, "STOP Playing by the Boys' Rules. The Game Is Rigged! 8 Ways to Play Your Own Game and FINALLY Make SUCCESS = HAPPINESS." Get it and learn more at www.RobinOnFire.com.

High Hair, High Hopes and Changing the World

Along the way I learned not to let anyone monkey with my swing

PATRICIA WYNN BROWN

Yes, I do think one person can change the world, but I wasn't absolutely clear as to how to do it early on. I really wanted to do it, one woman at a time, through comedy, raising spirits, helping people and making a joyful noise. Honestly, I think I'm doing it now, and so can you!

"Where there is woman, there is magic."
–Ntozake Shonge, playwright, performance artist, writer

[**Some simple instructions for the reader**: My Little Spit Curl, I will be telling you my story of following my bliss and how I am changing the world. Every so often I am throwing in a quote that has been meaningful to me as I head down the yellow brick road of passion seeking. These quotes are helpful little whoops of hope. And now back to our story.]

BUT FIRST, A LITTLE HISTORY LESSON

It probably all started with Annette Funicello, yes, Annette, the famous Mouseketeer from the REAL Mouseketeers in the 1950s. Added to this was a heavy dose of influence from my Aunt Pat, who was a professional ice skater. Seeing her in her heavenly sequined outfit with all that makeup and hairdo made me think: *This is how I want to dress for work.*

"I go forth alone and stand as ten thousand."
–Maya Angelou, in *Our Grandmothers*

I thought to my five-year-old self, how can I make this possible? I can't dance, I can't ice skate, I can't even make it clear to my family that I WANT TO BE IN SHOW BUSINESS. Everyone was busy.

"It is never too late to be what you might have been."
–George Eliot

It took only about 34 years but, in a way, now I *am* a Mousketeer (but not as gorgeous, congenial or talented as Annette or my Aunt Pat). What happened was this: dance classes were not in the cards for a struggling family of six, nor were acting lessons, or any of those things to prepare you for life as a Mouseketeer. Plus, I surmised that dreams came true for other girls, not me.

So I followed the more traditional track and made selections from the restricted career menu we were offered in 1969: housewife, teacher, nurse, secretary. I chose wife/mother/speech therapist/teacher.

At the age of 39, I started a new career as a writer and, eventually, a performer. I wrote a humor column for 10 years, and a book about parenting, and then I was asked to do speaking. Even though I wanted to be a performer, I had a terrible case of stage fright. As odd as this seems, I've learned it is more frequent with performers than you might guess. So as long as I had a bottle of Immodium with me, I was good to go with the speaking. (Fortunately, I'm Immodium-free these days.)

"If you don't take risks, you risk everything."
–Geena Davis

Then I decided to write my own style of one-woman shows (chit-chat performance) because then I wouldn't have to memorize any lines, which petrifies me, and I developed my own little way of staging these shows so I would always have an outline nearby (like Dumbo's feather) and would never have to worry about forgetting what comes next.

So I wrote a piece about kids growing up and out of the nest and then a piece about my adventures (I've had some really good adventures!), and then I was watching my hairdresser work one day, and I saw how she sort of counseled people and helped them achieve their hopes and dreams through little scraps of magazine photos of hairdos and how people told their hairdressers absolutely everything (and loudly, if they were under the hair dryer).

I thought to myself, *This would make a great performance piece.* As a result, I wrote the first episode of Hair Theater®, which I performed with three other women. In it, we told the stories of our lives through the evolution of our hairdos. It was a hit.

The first performance was in 2001. Since those days, it has become a one-woman show with about eight episodes, revolving around different themes. They include a cancer survivor episode, a Catholic School Girl episode ("Hair Folly-cles at Our Lady of Perpetually Glorious Hairdos High") and a heart-health awareness episode. There is even a "hairy-aoke" sing-along version of Hair Theater.

Just ask a woman about her hairdo history and she can fill you in on her best hairdos and worst hairdos and that awful perm and what her mother did to her bangs and what she did to her sister's hair in the name of beauty and style and what happened with her prom or wedding hair.

My tip to psychologists: Ask your patient to bring in a significant hairdo photo and describe what's happening on her head and in her life. Very revealing! Laughter and tears prevail.

> *"If you can make an audience cry then make them laugh,*
> *then you've done your job."*
> **–Jackie Gleason**

So the show started rolling along in all of its manifestations, but I had to conquer some obstacles along the way. These included but were not limited to: fear of failure, naysayers, marketing challenges, lack of interest in others, logistical hell in bringing performances into production, unreliable people, nature, starting a new endeavor like this at my age, juggling my family responsibilities with shows and travel, money, money, money, and hushing those voices in my head that would love it if I would just give it all up and become a greeter at Wal-Mart (which I consider a noble profession, and I would be very, very good at it).

"Talent's helpful, but guts are absolutely necessary."
–Jessamyn West

SOLUTIONS

My Little Spit Curl Reader, the aforementioned problems that are associated with *any* new and different endeavor are inevitable; if they weren't, everyone would be Annette Funicello and my Aunt Pat. So if you are going to follow your bliss, read some Joseph Campbell theology/mythology books and get to work. Mouseketeers don't grow on trees, you know.

"If you follow your bliss, you put yourself on a kind of track that has been there all the while waiting for you and the life that you ought to be living is the one you are living. Wherever you are—if you are following your bliss, you are enjoying that refreshment—that life within you, all the time."
–Joseph Campbell

Grow up! Problems are part and parcel of the process. You got your dreams. You got your problems. What's the problem? Solve 'em. Got it?

One thing that helps me so much with the problem areas of following my hopes and dreams of changing the world is reading biographies and memoirs. Once you read a slew of these, it is very clear that the trick to success is getting back up once you get knocked down and learning from your mistakes. And as Ted Williams, the famous baseball player, once said, "Never let anyone monkey with your swing."

Here's what's meant by that: Say you have a dream and people keep wanting to reshape it, turn it into something else, or talk you out of it all together. If in your heart of hearts you really, truly, with everything that's in you believe in that dream, then don't let anyone (not even your mother or Simon Cowell) monkey with it.

Stay true to your school, and your bliss.

The other thing that helps is if you connect with people who get what you're trying to do. At *Women on Fire* we do that through tea parties, coaching and conferences. Not everyone is brave enough to be in the bliss following business, and changing the world appears daunting to those who enjoy the false comfort and stagnation of denying their inner Mouseketeers. Finding people who are not afraid to stop being afraid, and talking with them and drinking tea with them is your ticket to dramatic world changing results!

"Isolation is a dream killer."
–Barbara Sher, author, business owner, career counselor

Another huge help in following your bliss involves opening your eyes and seeing the sequins and beautiful sparkly eye shadow right before your very eyes. What is going on in your life that you are thankful for? (Right now, Spit Curl, name five.) It's enough to make you *wiggle your ears, like good Mouseketeers!*

And there's this: Put yourself in time out. Set the timer for 20 minutes and just sit there. Meditate. Listen to some beautiful music. Draw a picture. Pray. Watch the snow fall. Time out is magic. Try it. Inspiration is as close as your couch.

AND THEN SOMETIMES THE ICE MELTS

My friend noticed this little mole. I didn't give it a thought. She is a nurse and said I should get it checked. So I did. It was 1997, three years before I wrote the first installment of Hair Theater.

About a month after the doctor's appointment, the results came back and I sat in an oncologist's office. The nurse came in with me. She grabbed my hand. I thought, "Uh-Oh." The doctor told me I had malignant melanoma. I didn't have a clue what he was talking about. He said that's cancer. Good thing the nurse was holding my hand because the doc was clearly monkeying with my swing.

"You gain strength, courage, and confidence by every experience in which you really stop and look fear in the face...
you must do the thing you cannot do."
–Eleanor Roosevelt

Here is the honest to God's truth: The first thing I thought about was losing my hair. The second thing I thought about was death, in that order.

But I didn't lose my hair. And, I lived!!!!!!!!!!!!!!!!!!!

This is where the Hair Theater story gets a wee bit cloudy. Some people think I wrote Hair Theater as a result of my cancer and fear of hair loss. I didn't (consciously). I wrote the show because of my fascination with hair, hairdressers, our identities interwoven into our hair, and, frankly, women are very funny when it comes to their relationship with their hairdos (whether it's there or not, hers or store bought).

Because our paths are nothing if not interesting in how things tend to work out better than we plan, something began in 2001 with the Hair Theater show that has helped me to change the world, one woman at a time.

"A person should set his goals as early as he can and devote all his energy and talent to getting there. With enough effort, he may achieve it. Or he may find something that is even more rewarding. But in the end, no matter what the outcome, he will know he has been alive.
–Walt Disney

GIVING

I knew I wanted to be able to do some good with my professional work to benefit others. The comment I most enjoy with the performances is: "I needed that laugh more than you'll ever know." My second favorite remark is: "I laughed so hard my face hurts." Love that!

There was more to be done in changing the world in addition to raising its spirits, and that's how the Hair Theater Fund at the Columbus Foundation got its start. With the help of some wonderful volunteers (including our own cheerleading troupe that performs Ambush Pep Rallies for women/kids going through chemo), along with fund advocates, and generous donors, this fund is definitely changing the world one woman at a time.

The Hair Theater Fund was established to assist women in financial need in Central Ohio with wigs and/or hats, necessitated by chemotherapy. It started with a white envelope and about $200 that I took to the Over My Head wig shop in Columbus and explained to the then owner, Carol Hoyt, that I wanted to use a percentage of my performance fees to help women with wigs.

About this time I met with a friend who was offering me some career advice, and she asked me what my goal was with the fund. I told her that if any woman, in financial need, medically treated in my county, needed a wig, the fund would provide it.

She thought that was a stretch. It wasn't a stretch. It was my swing.

"Our doubts are traitors and make us lose the good we oft might win by fearing to attempt."
–Shakespeare

DIVINE INTERVENTION

Those who know me understand that I am a huge proponent of Irish Catholic Voodoo, and by this I mean no disrespect. I adore the saints and angels, am a true fan of the BVM (Blessed Virgin Mary); I sleep with my rosary and regularly commune with St. Anthony (patron saint of lost objects) when it comes to my keys and reading glasses.

That explains what happens next.

Did you know that you cannot really donate money from a white envelope on a regular basis and have that be tax friendly? News to me.

I had not one clue as to how to proceed and not land in prison for changing the world one woman at a time with funny money.

"You will do foolish things, but do them with enthusiasm."
–Colette

Let's just go back to my SAT scores for a moment, shall we? High verbal. Lower than low math. With all the meetings about money and 501c3's and payment systems to hospitals, and accounting spreadsheets and talking with people about the statistical need for wigs in the community (which was an ordeal to find out anything about)… and hours and hours of trying to change the world one woman at a time that was coming to nothing, I had had it.

Fortunately for me, I live my life in reverse so since dance classes were not in our family budget when I was a child, I take them now. One Saturday morning I was getting ready for ballet class and I put on my tights. I had been through another grueling week of trying to change the world and there just didn't seem to be a solution and I was going to throw in the hairbrush and not do the wig fund.

I slipped my foot into the ballet tights. There was something hard in the toe. Assuming the worst (water bug?) I jumped out of the tights faster that you can say Meeska-Mooska. I pulled the hard thing out and it was a medal of the Virgin Mary, a medal that neither my husband nor I owned. I kid you not, as Jack Paar would say.

Just then it felt like a huge load had been lifted off my shoulders. It was palpable.

> *"God will not have his work made manifest by cowards."*
> **–Ralph Waldo Emerson**

By chance the following Monday, I spoke with attorney Nancy Koerner, and she was the one who helped me work through all of the legal, financial and math problems. I started a "donor specified fund." It was a perfect solution. Nancy was my angel.

Note: There are angels everywhere. Make sure you leave some pixie dust out for them!

HERE'S WHAT I'M TALKING ABOUT

Maybe you don't think making people laugh or getting them wigs when they can't afford them can change the world. Believe me it does. Our "Star Wig Recipients" tell me so.

What about this word problem, you math Wiz': So a woman comes to the show in a terrible mood. Maybe she thinks her life is a mess and nothing good will happen for her. Maybe she has a great idea to change the world but she is discouraged because there is too much math involved and money is always Problem Number One on almost everyone's list, and that makes it all seem insurmountable, and people would feel a whole lot better if she behaved as usual and DID NOT ROCK THE BOAT for goodness sake. Still and all, she wants to rock the boat, but she knows if she rocks it, people will get upset or seasick.

"In a world not made for women, criticism and ridicule follow us all the days of our lives. Usually they are indications that we are doing something right."
–Erica Jong, in *Fear of Fifty*

So this fledgling rebel audience woman watches a Hair Theater episode, and it strikes a chord with her and she laughs and laughs so hard that her face hurts. It hurts so good. Then her spirits lift and she feels a sense of possibility and then she feels a little braver and remembers that she has a friend who can do math she can count on and another friend who understands what she's trying to do to change the world, and she joins the *Women on Fire*™ to build her strategies and resolve, and she sees this performer (that would be me) get up there and do her thing with *NO DISCERNIBLE TALENT* or ice-skating prowess or Mouseketeer-level skills and yet, *somehow her wacky stories and antics and world views work.*

"Dry, she ain't much. Wet, she's a star!"
–Movie producer, Harry Cohn, about Esther Williams

And then our struggling audience member says the magic words that she learned from the *Wizard of Oz* movie, *If happy little blue birds fly/ beyond the rainbow/ why....oh....why...can't....I—I-I-I-I-I-I-I-I-I-I.*
And you know what, My Little Spit Curl? She can.

SCHINDLER'S LIST

A line in the movie *Schindler's List* sticks with me through all of my efforts to change the world. The line is, "If you save one life, you save the world entire."

At every performance and speech that I give, I tell the audience that there is at least one person there who needs to go to the doctor for a check up or to get something they are concerned about examined. They are either putting it off, or afraid to go, or forgetting to take care of themselves, or or or or or, you know the score. It is a clarion call for early detection of any medical or emotional problems.

And you know what, My Little Spit Curl? Someone always goes. And so, at every show, I save a life. (Maybe you need to go. Do you? If so…do.) This call to action takes about three minutes out of the show. You can change the world in three minutes. I have.

HOW TO CHANGE THE WORLD (IN 38 WORDS)

The world isn't changed through huge seismic shifts of grandiose gestures. It is changed with one smile, one act of kindness, one step toward your goals, one strong conviction that the dreams of your youth need never fade.

TIMETABLE FOR CHANGING THE WORLD

Got three minutes?

"To dare, progress is at this price."
–Victor Hugo, in *Les Miserables*

PATRICIA WYNN BROWN performs Hair Theater® episodes across the United States. She has written two books: *Hair-A-Baloo: The Revealing Comedy and Tragedy on Top of Your Head* and *Momma Culpa: One Woman Comes Clean and Makes Her Maternal Confession.* She is a three-time winner of the James Thurber Summer Writing Contest and was a featured humorist in the PBS documentary about Erma Bombeck. She and her husband have been an item since the LBJ administration and have a son.

Acknowledgements

My name may be on the cover of this book, but I am deeply indebted and grateful to my 19 partners on this project. They are the chapter authors, the courageous women who boldly opened their hearts and shared their struggles and strategies because they want to ease the way for other women.

To each one: You are awesome and an inspiration. I love you!

From the day she sent it, I regularly reread author and stand-up comic Janette Barber's gracious Foreword as inspiration to live up to her praise. You must meet her because you will want her as your best friend.

In addition to the writers, many wonderful, enthusiastic supporters created a force-field around me that led to the unfolding of the Women on Fire™ movement and to this book.

Thank you to my best friend, Jan Allen, for endless hours over three decades to "figure out life" and for encouraging me always. And to Nancy Neal, my spiritual sister and angel: I owe much to my former boyfriend (now your husband!) for introducing us.

I am extremely grateful to the two women whose works led me to create my own version of Women on Fire™: Filmmaker Kathleen Laughlin made the delightful documentary movie *Woman on Fire: Menopause Stories*. And author, poet and performer Irene O'Garden wrote the much-acclaimed and captivating one-woman play *Women on*

Fire. They are phenomenally talented and generous women, and Irene, in particular, inspired and encouraged me.

Alexandria Brown opened up an important channel for me when I joined her elite mastermind group and she introduced me to Christine Kloser, an author herself and publisher of Love Your Life Publishing. Thank you, Christine and team, including the very talented designer Sarah Van Male and the engaging Marlene Oulton who was always eager and ready to help.

In the final months, I relied on Kacy Cook, an extraordinarily gifted editor and writer and a lifelong friend, who swooped in, dug deep and worked shoulder-to-shoulder with me to refine and finish this book. She is first-rate in every way.

Hugs and kisses to the "A" team: Andrea Dowding and Angela Ittu for infinite inspiration, strategies and support; Mandy Pratt for exquisite connections; Meredith Paige for filmmaking; Shannon McCaffery for photography and marketing; and Holly Getty for all-things-style and blissful comfort at the Holly Day Inn.

I am blessed that Blue Cullen is our every thing at the office, and Regina Blos is our glue at home.

Every coach needs a safe, inspiring haven to take extremely good care of herself. I found mine in Denise Guest and Yvette Peterson.

Special thanks to these invaluable supporters: Arnold Adoff, Ryan and Sarah Ausley, Robin Baliszewski, Edward Beck, Dr. Constance Berkley, Kelly Boggs, Liz Boyd, Alan Brigish, Debbie Brown, Barry Brown, Cindy Brown, Christopher, Elle, Max and Julia Celeste, Dagmar Celeste, Debbie Cook, Melissa Daimler, MJ Bindu Delekta, Carolyn Ellis, Laura and Ted Federici, Anne Gallagher, Bill Glazer, Ann Graham, Stedman Graham, Jennifer Granholm, Joe and Jennifer Gregg, Joe and Susan Henson, Randy Kamen-Gredinger, Tama Kieves, Dr. Elvira Lang, Jenifer Madson, Priscilla Mead, Claudia Miller, Erin Moriarty, Daniel Granholm Mulhern, Gina Otto, Elaine Pace, Ranjana Pathak, Ellen Pearlman, Dianne and Scott Phillips, Steve, Gaby, Ashley and Jordan Phillips, Penny Rhodes, Maureen Riopelle, Mary Jo Ruggieri, Sherrie Russell, Kit and Ray Sawyer, Barbara Sher, Peter and Ronni Simon, Karen Skurka, Agapi Stassinopoulos, Curt Steiner, Gail Straub, Bob and Lucinda Sweeney, Diane Torrisi, Penelope Trunk, Ellen Wingard and

Jodie Wright.

I honor the members of the first Women on Fire™ coaching group, led by Andrea Dowding in Columbus, Ohio: Jenn Bajec, Patricia Wynn Brown, Noelle Celeste, Robin Leonard, Julie Moorehead, Kitty Munger, Tandi Phillips Musuraca and Christine Wagner.

At Lady Mendl's in New York City, we've held tea parties and events since 2004 and have been rewarded with excellent service led by Shawn Rettstatt and "Tea Captain" James Galaites.

Much love and credit goes to the original Woman on Fire in my life: my mother, Mary Lue Phillips. You are a grand personality and a tremendous inspiration!

Most important of all, I bow to my husband and business partner, Rob Berkley. You have calmed me down, lifted me up and given me all the love and support possible to pursue my dreams and vision. I love you. And given that the brilliant tea party idea was yours, I promise to let you attend one some day!

And, finally, to every girl and woman I've ever shared an authentic, intimate conversation with about love, loss, life, hopes and dreams, you know who you are. This book is for you.

An Invitation from Debbie

I'm thrilled you found your way to us!

Right now you may be wondering what your own next steps are to being on fire with your life. As a favorite teacher of mine, Marianne Williamson, says, "Don't stop now, before the miracle happens!"

If what you've read so far and the 20 Women on Fire™ Aspirations in the front of this book speak to you, you may want to consider joining us. There are many opportunities for you to connect and thrive in the Women on Fire™ community.

I would be honored to have you join our ever-expanding circle!

Here are a few ways to be involved:

- Become a member of Women on Fire™. With membership, you will receive monthly newsletters full of inspiration, strategies and support to help you keep your fire burning bright. You'll also receive an audio CD each month featuring an inspiring woman who will share her wisdom and more. You will find us at: www.BeAWomanOnFire.com

- Attend a Women on Fire™ tea party in your area. To be notified of events and tea parties, please join our mailing list at: www.BeAWomanOnFire.com

If you are an experienced coach or facilitator and would like to learn more about hosting Women on Fire™ tea parties or coaching groups in your area, please contact us at Info@BeAWomanOnFire.com

- While I no longer coach individual women on an ongoing basis, I do lead a small number of group and private Vision Days each year.

- I also have a limited membership, private coaching group. If you would like to be considered for Vision Day or for future membership in the Founder's Coaching Group, please contact us for an application at Info@BeAWomanOnFire.com

Thank you for your interest.

Here's to living a life you are on fire about!

Love,
Debbie

Contact

DEBBIE PHILLIPS

Founder, Women on Fire™

Address: PO Box 786, West Tisbury, MA   02575
Phone: (508) 696-4949
Email: Info@BeAWomanOnFire.com
Main website: www.BeAWomanOnFire.com
Other websites:
www.AboutWomenOnFire.com
www.WomenOnFireMembers.com
www.VisionDay.com
www.GriefRelief.com

ONLINE

Blog: www.DebbiePhillips.com
Twitter: WomanonFire
Facebook: Go to: Debbie Phillips and request to join the private group Women on Fire™
YouTube: Subscribe and receive video tips and information at www.youtube.com/beawomanonfire

For quantity book sales or to sponsor a Women on Fire event in your area, please call (508) 696-4949.

About Debbie Phillips

Debbie Phillips is the inspiring founder of Women on Fire™ and a pioneer in the field of executive and life coaching. She is known for her work transforming women's lives.

In 1995, Debbie created a service for leaders and women in transition that previously didn't exist but that she had wished for earlier in her career. Executive and life coaching were all but unheard of in professional circles at the time, and she was among the first trained coaches in the world.

After several years of coaching individuals and teams, she founded Women on Fire™, an organization that features tea parties, retreats and coaching groups to extend the outreach of support for women's success.

Debbie also created and co-developed Vision Day˙, a strategic planning day that has helped thousands of people live the lives they've dreamed of.

Prior to becoming a coach, she was a reporter for the *Columbus (Ohio) Citizen-Journal*; a deputy press secretary to former U.S. Senator John Glenn during his quest for the Democratic presidential nomination; press secretary to former Ohio Governor Richard F. Celeste; and an executive with U.S. Health Productions Co., which featured the internationally syndicated television health and lifestyle show *Life Choices with Erie Chapman*.

Debbie has a bachelor's degree in journalism from The Ohio State University and a master's degree in public administration from the John F. Kennedy School of Government at Harvard University.

She and her husband and collaborator, Rob Berkley, live with their big white cat, Wilber, on Martha's Vineyard, Mass., and in Naples, Fla.